To Jill
Best Wishes
Lilian Chamber

Mrs C. In Residence

Mrs C. In Residence

Lilian Chamberlain

The Pentland Press Limited
Edinburgh • Cambridge • Durham • USA

© Lilian Chamberlain 1997

First published in 1997 by
The Pentland Press Ltd.
1 Hutton Close
South Church
Bishop Auckland
Durham

All rights reserved.
Unauthorised duplication
contravenes existing laws.

British Library Cataloguing in Publication Data.
A Catalogue record for this book is available
from the British Library.

ISBN 1 85821 526 9

Typeset by CBS, Felixstowe, Suffolk
Printed and bound by Bookcraft Ltd., Bath

To my husband Bernard, without whose encouragement and support this book would never have been written, and to my grandchildren, Josie and Steven.

FOREWORD

by Bernard Chamberlain.

For eighteen years I succeeded in leading a double life without attracting unwelcome attention. Outwardly I was just an ordinary teacher and, later, headmaster. But when school finished for the day, I didn't travel to a traditional suburban semi. I lived in a Residential Home for the Elderly. It was the only way I could be with my wife, who wrote this book. The conditions of her employment at that time meant that she, and therefore I, had to be in residence at the Homes where she worked.

The accommodation for residential staff was in such close proximity to the residents' quarters, that I gained a valuable insight into the workings of Homes, as will readers of this book.

Ever since I have known her, Lilian has been a very caring sort of person, but, she realised, that to be of practical help in caring for others, she had to supplement her own experience and natural instincts by undertaking relevant training. So, at an age when many would be content to remain a wife and mother (in both of which spheres she was admirable), Lilian spent much time and energy in gaining qualifications which enabled her to be in a position where she could really influence the care – in its widest sense – of many elderly people.

Of course, she had the support of many members of staff, some of whom, as will be revealed in the book, were initially as set in their ways as the residents, 'set' being an appropriate word. Residents were wakened early, herded down for communal breakfast, then into lounges where they adorned the walls, dozing until the midday meal. The afternoon and evening followed a similar pattern until the residents were probably exhausted by boredom and ready for bed.

Unfortunately, in some Homes this sort of regime still applies, and obviously some residents are physically and mentally unable to benefit from much else. But, as again will be shown in this book, Homes can be interesting, even exciting, for residents and staff.

My own colleagues were mildly amused at where I lived. The children accepted it readily enough; they probably thought it was a suitable place for someone of my advanced years. Most of the Homes' residents knew what my occupation was. However, as was shown by a conversation I overheard, some thought I was just a lazy member of their staff. When two ladies I had taken up in the lift thought they were out of earshot, one said to the other, 'That chap always seems to be dashing in and out but you never see him doing any proper work, do you? I don't know what he gets paid for.'

Well, I wasn't paid to do anything in the Homes but, carried along by Lilian's enthusiasm and commitment, I became involved in various activities from time to time. I enjoyed hearing about what had happened each day and Lilian, apparently, enjoyed hearing about what had been going on in school. We used to laugh sometimes that our lives and attention seemed to be centred around elderly people and children. But there is often an affinity between those two age groups, so perhaps our differing occupations and particular interests had something in common.

Reading this book provided me with a pleasant stroll down memory lane. Many readers could find it an informative account of life in Homes, something that affects an increasing number of people, with a colourful background of true incidents and anecdotes. Of course, I'm biased, but I enjoyed reading it. I hope that you will find it equally rewarding.

CHAPTER I

Walking up the short driveway, I paused to look at the building I was approaching. Brick-built, occupying the width of half-a-dozen houses and with two upper floors, it resembled a small block of rather pleasant flats. Even the modest inscription above the doorway, George Moore Lodge, gave no indication of its real purpose.

A discerning observer might have noticed the collection of high-backed chairs grouped in one large room. The people sitting in them gave the final clue. It was an Old People's Home.

Opening my handbag, I fingered the long buff envelope containing the letter inviting me for interview as the part-time Clerk for the Home. Had I been wise to apply for this job? How many others were being considered? A dozen similar thoughts and questions raced around my head. As I pushed open the front door and stepped into the hallway, I little realised that this was the symbolic entrance into a completely new phase of my life, which was to last for eighteen years.

Having recently moved from Essex to London, I had been feeling rather unsettled, not knowing quite what to do with myself. My husband, a teacher, was fully occupied most of the time; our son was at school studying for GCE exams. Browsing through the local newspaper, I noticed an advertisement: 'Part-time Clerk required for Old People's Home.'

Sounded interesting! Just the sort of job I would like. The money would come in handy, too!

On the application form, I listed my previous experiences, ranging from dressmaking and factory war work to reception/filing clerk in a solicitors' office. In addition I was able to mention voluntary hospital and Red Cross work, YMCA youth club leadership, plus being a helper at blind and old people's clubs. Quite an assortment. Would my prospective employers at the Town Hall find something there to interest them, I wondered?

The letter I was now holding had provided confirmation of that. Four of us were being considered for the post, and I was delighted when it was offered to me. I commenced my duties in the summer of 1967.

The lady from the Town Hall who had interviewed me, had warned that things would be difficult to begin with. The Home had no permanent staff in charge at that time, waiting for vacancies to be filled. There was just a succession of nurses, coming and going on a temporary basis. Whilst they were able to cope with the medical side of things, they hadn't a clue about all the other tasks involved.

There were times in those early days when I wondered what I had let myself in for. My main duties were to deal with the residents' pensions, pass invoices, do the accounts and staff weekly time sheets, answer the phone and be a receptionist.

No one could show me what to do, and apart from a few hours spent with a clerk from another Home, I had to muddle along, finding out things for myself. However, because of this situation, I quickly familiarised myself with residents, staff and the geography of the building. That familiarity and all it encompassed was to remain with me for eight years.

The corridors of the building were very wide, as were the doors. The floor was tiled, and I remember feeling conscious of the clatter and echo of my shoes when I was walking around. The lounges were large and impersonal, although they did have carpets. On the ground floor were two lounges with elderly women all sitting round the walls. Most spent their time nodding off to sleep. Where were the men? On the ground floor there was also a smaller lounge for visitors and other activities; and a large kitchen and communal dining-room, medical and sick rooms, office, staff room, utility room and toilets.

The elusive men were to be found on the middle floor. They were the sole occupants of the one large lounge. I clearly recall the first time I popped my head round that door to greet them with a bright and breezy, 'Good morning, gentlemen.'

Stony silence followed. Then one old chap enquired of another, 'Oo the . . . 'ell is she?' Whoops! Bang went my pre-conceived notion that all the residents would be dear old souls. It seemed I was in for a surprise or two.

The rest of the middle floor consisted of bedrooms, toilets, bathrooms and a two-bedroom staff flat. The residents' bedrooms were mostly shared by two, three or four, although there were a few for single occupancy. The top floor was similar in layout, minus the lounge. There was a very wide staircase, but also a lift, the scene of an amusing incident several years after I first came to the Home. By that time my husband and I were living there ourselves – not as residents, but because I had become the Matron.

One of the residents, Laura Venables, had entrusted me with a great secret, which I assured her would remain in confidence as far as I was concerned. A few weeks later I received an urgent summons to one of the communal lounges, where Laura was slumped in an armchair, complaining of dizziness. Having decided it would be wise to take her to the bedroom, I lifted her into a wheelchair. Because it was evening and few staff were on duty, my husband, Bernard, who happened to be passing, helped me.

The lift was too small to accommodate all of us, so I walked ahead up the stairs, leaving Bernard to take Miss Venables in the lift. Whirring upwards it stopped abruptly at the next level. Indeed the stop was so violent that despite Bernard's grip on the chair, it shot forward a couple of inches. The unconscious Laura jerked forward, too. To Bernard's horror, that unexpected movement appeared to cause Laura's head to fall off. In growing panic he reached for the button to open the lift doors. I was able to convince him that the old lady was unharmed, although there was something distinctly odd and eerie about her appearance. I knew the reason, and Bernard soon understood it, too.

Miss Venables's secret was out, or rather down, on the floor of the lift – a luxuriant, auburn wig.

After I had been working in the Home for a few months, a Superintendent was appointed to take charge of it. One of the temporary nurses stayed on as Matron. At last we would have some stability in the establishment.

Arthur, the newly-appointed Superintendent, was a very short, stout, bespectacled man, with light gingery hair and the kind of freckles common to people of that colouring. Having been in charge of another Home before coming to George Moore Lodge, he was very experienced. Despite feeling a trifle apprehensive at first – as one usually does with a new colleague – I soon discovered there was nothing to worry about, and that we shared a similar sense of humour. Arthur was a kind and caring man, producing the instinctive feeling that the residents would be in good hands. It was indeed fortunate that he had come to George Moore Lodge, for a very happy working relationship and lasting friendship developed between us.

CHAPTER II

Quite suddenly, after I had been the Clerk for nearly two years, the Matron announced that she was leaving for personal reasons, and thus her post, which was really that of Deputy to the Superintendent, became vacant.

One afternoon, Arthur, the Superintendent, made a rather surprising remark to me. 'Why don't you apply for the Matron's post? You would be ideal, and I can't think of anyone I would rather have as my deputy.'

By that time I had become very involved in all aspects of the Home and was very interested in the work. So, with the encouraging remarks of the Superintendent still ringing in my ears, I returned home that day to discuss the suggestion with Bernard and our son, Steven. He was a teenager, soon to start College.

In those days it was a condition of employment that Senior staff should live on the premises, so this was not simply taking up another job. We would have to sell our house and go to live in at the Home. We discussed all the implications, then Bernard and Steven agreed that I should 'have a go'. They knew how committed I had become to this interesting and worthwhile work. So with their support and encouragement I applied.

Anxious days of waiting followed, until I was eventually short-listed, interviewed by the Assistant Director and members of the Committee, and offered the post. We sold our house and moved in to the top floor flat. Now my induction to residential work was really about to begin, and privacy was to become a thing of the past. One night, for example, an old lady walked into our flat and tried to get into bed with us!

The diversity of duties in my new post required skills and knowledge I had not even suspected I possessed. Housekeeping on the grand scale was called for, with making up orders for food, cleaning materials and similar items, as well as checking the requirements for the repair and maintenance of furnishings and domestic equipment such as refrigerators.

When the GPs made their calls I metaphorically put on a nurse's uniform to discuss medicines and treatment for sick residents. In other areas of medical territory, I assisted the chiropodist and arranged appointments for residents to be seen by the dentist and the optician.

As a temporary surveyor, I checked requirements for the repair and maintenance of the building itself. Back in the office there were numerous forms to be filled in and reports to be written. An aptitude for accountancy was needed when budgeting, without the advantage of using calculators which were not yet in vogue.

Sometimes I had to don the cook's apron when no one else was available. I hope my culinary efforts did not speed the departure of any of the residents. In short, I was concerned with everything catering for the residents' welfare, from the time they were admitted to our Home until the time they departed, almost invariably to that even larger Home in the sky.

However, a few years in the post made me feel the need to learn more by taking a full-time training course. My local authority seconded me and in 1973 I obtained the Certificate in Residential Social Work. A temporary Matron had been employed in the Home to help Arthur whilst I was at College.

Prior to my training I just drifted along on the tide, believing as many others did, that old people needed to be cosseted and 'cared for'. I guess this was a natural assumption to make, following on the heels of the dreaded workhouse. The authorities were trying to right what had seemed a terrible wrong, and in the process went from one extreme to the other. George Moore Lodge was a very good Home of its kind, so in those very early days I had no cause to question whether it was right or wrong to create such dependency.

At the time of my original appointment, the Homes had been administered by separate Health and Welfare Committees. Later the administration was in the hands of the Social Services Committee. The terms 'Social Services' and 'Social Worker', so much in evidence today, then came into use.

In 1955 the Ministry of Health had recommended that units for sixty elderly people should be built. George Moore Lodge was obviously one such establishment. Some years later this was changed to an emphasis on smaller units.

All these Homes were referred to as 'Part 3 ' and at College I was soon to learn that this arose from Part 3 of the 1948 National Assistance Act which stated that local authorities were 'required to provide residential care for all persons who, by reason of age, infirmity or any other circumstances, are in need of care not otherwise available to them.' Hooray! At last I knew the meaning of 'Part 3 '.

Before the war, and indeed up to the implementation of the 1948 legislation, old or infirm people who lacked the means to pay for private care and who had no one to care for them, often ended their days in places which had previously been workhouses. Many retained characteristics of their former purpose. The use of the term 'infirmary', too, was an indication of the condition of many earlier occupants of institutions still bearing that name.

My training opened up many opportunities for new experiences. Every minute was valuable for me, although we had to work very hard and it was very exhausting. However, it did serve to make me see the future more clearly and the part I must play in helping to implement a more progressive and less institutional type of care for the elderly. It became my ambition to be in charge of a Home myself one day, thereby being in a better position to influence others.

The 1948 act had heralded improvements in conditions for the elderly and infirm by making it incumbent upon local authorities to make specific provision for these people. What a pity that the authorities were not also required to provide sufficient staff to implement the new style of care being advocated! Staffing levels were very poor; and in some establishments today they still are.

At the time I took up my Matron's post, the Homes usually had just two people in charge, called Superintendent or Matron according to their sex. Often they were husband and wife.

The overall administration and supervision for the running of George Moore Lodge fell to Arthur, myself and the part-time Clerk who had taken over my previous duties. In addition, it must be realised that such an establishment requires the provision of care for the residents twenty-four hours daily, seven days a week.

Our immediate support in looking after the residents came from Attendants, as they were called at that time. Like us, they had to work varying shifts to provide the necessary whole-time cover. Then there were Domestics, employed mainly for cleaning duties and helping in the kitchen, a couple of part-time Cooks and a part-time Handyman/Gardener.

The Attendants were categorised as male and female Attendants, the idea being that they would attend to the special needs of men or women residents. Whilst obviously there might be some merit in having certain Attendants designated to cater for the needs of men where they differed from women (shaving them, for example) this was just part of a firmly entrenched and somewhat artificial segregation, which would not be found in one's own home. Another example of it was the separate lounges.

One of many improvements in recent years is that Attendants are now more usually called Care Assistants. This might seem a trivial matter, but it is one small indication of a considerable change of attitude that has come about. The word 'Attendant' (despite the fact that many worthy people doing useful jobs are described in that way) gives a less accurate picture than 'Care Assistant' of the work that helpers in Homes are doing. It seems a more friendly description for those who are indeed employed to care for and assist the elderly residents.

An indication of the inadequate staffing levels referred to earlier was the fact that there was only one Attendant on waking duty throughout the night to deal with sixty residents. This meant that invariably Arthur or I (whichever one of us was on sleeping-in duty) would be called up during the night. On many occasions it would be just to assist with lifting a resident on to the toilet, when the Attendant could not manage this on her own.

One recalls that not only were the hours of duty much longer in those days, but we didn't even get paid for overtime we worked or for sleeping-in duties. On reflection, it seems we were thoroughly exploited.

CHAPTER III

About the time I finished my training there was an awakening to the importance of the emotional needs of residents, and changes were beginning to take place.

Our manual staff establishment hours were increased, allowing the employment of two waking staff for nights. We were also able to engage another full-time and part-time Assistant Matron. This made an enormous difference, giving the opportunity for the implementation of some ideas which at that time were considered to be more progressive.

It was now possible to hold more staff meetings and do some training to try to ensure that everyone was pulling in the same direction. We tackled the segregation of men and women in the lounges mentioned earlier. It was also agreed that more effort should be put into stimulating and motivating the residents through activities such as an art class and a story reading group.

Initially many of the staff had to be convinced of the value of such changes. However, the chief difficulty was that the residents had become so dependent on having everything done for them that they had virtually lost the ability to think for themselves. It was quite an uphill struggle, and the constraints of the building itself didn't help either.

The Attendants were mostly middle aged and very hard-working women. Occasionally younger male Attendants worked in the Home for a while; but they never seemed to stay long. Of all the Attendants, one stood out as a real treasure; Millie Liam. She had worked in the Home from the day it opened.

Millie was a real-life version of the popular fictional type – a rough diamond with a heart of gold beneath her gruff exterior. Most Homes have a 'character' on the staff, and Millie was certainly ours. She was so dependable and such a born leader that the other Attendants automatically went to her for guidance. However, and perhaps a trifle surprisingly for someone who stood out for her many good points, Millie had one pronounced fault. She took very little pride in her appearance. Overalls were worn by Attendants at that time. Hers always contrived to look grubby even when fresh on.

Arthur had mentioned this to her on several occasions, with no effect, so he asked me to try a woman to woman approach. I invited Millie into the office where we chatted generally for a few minutes; then I came straight to the point, and explained that her casual attitude about her appearance was a source of embarrassment for us, as it reflected badly on standards in the Home. She took it very well. Perhaps she hadn't thought about the matter in that way before. To her credit, from then on she always looked neat and tidy.

A special bond was forged between us that day. Later we discovered a coincidence that seemed to strengthen that link; we were the same age and our birthdays were on the same day.

As George Moore Lodge was situated in one of the London Boroughs, several members of staff were black. Our own house contains a number of souvenirs brought back by some of them as gifts for me, from places such as Jamaica.

One evening two black Attendants knocked frantically on the door of my flat on the top floor of the Home. They were terribly distraught. When they had tried to bath one of the residents, Mrs Jones, she had ordered them, 'Take your black hands off me!'

Calming them down, I explained that she had not actually meant to insult them. The elderly folk we were caring for, had grown up with all the old misconceived prejudices about 'coloured' people, and retained them. At such a late stage in their lives it was difficult for them to suddenly acquire more enlightened opinions.

Whilst the two Attendants went away to think about what I had said, I made haste to confront Mrs Jones. As I had tried to persuade the staff to understand the reason for the old lady's remark, I now told her to put herself in their position. How cruel she had been to those girls who were there to care for her. What would she do without the help of the staff, whatever their colour?

Mrs Jones quickly appreciated how she would have felt if someone had spoken to her in such a hurtful way, and she wanted to express her sorrow by apologising, which she duly did. For their part they accepted the apology. However, for some time after this, I made a point of discreetly observing them all as I didn't want any further recriminations.

Happily I noticed that the staff and Mrs Jones seemed to develop a new kind of acceptance and tolerance of each other. Such an incident had seemed almost inevitable, and by clearing the air I felt a better understanding had been promoted on both sides.

Late on another evening there was urgent knocking at the flat door. This time it was Miss Potter, one of the night Attendants. She was the sort of large, lovable black lady whose appearance suggested she could have stepped straight out of one of many films in that period depicting the American South. Now her normally sunny countenance was replaced on this occasion by a look combining anger and disbelief.

With eyes nearly popping out of her head she indignantly reported that when she had gone into Mr Conway's room to give him his night medication, he had thrust an envelope into her hand, telling her to read it when she finished her rounds.

Slipping the envelope in her overall pocket, she thought no more about it until she sat down to have a cup of tea. When she opened the envelope she found two one pound notes inside, with a message scribbled on a piece of paper. It said, 'Come into my room tonight so that I can have a feel of your . . .' At this, the words stopped short. The old chap had obviously forgotten what he did want a feel of. But the two pounds was for her services.

Although I could not help but see an element of humour in the situation, I realised that Miss Potter was insulted, and understandably so. To placate her, I told her to leave the letter and the money with me, with the assurance that I would speak severely to Mr Conway about it next morning.

Back in my own bed I gave way to laughter, and after explaining to Bernard what had happened, we both toyed with the idea that I should impersonate Miss Potter and go into Mr Conway's room, just for the devilment of finding out his reaction.

However, next morning I had to adopt my Matron's stance when asking Mr Conway to come into the office. He was such a tiny little fellow that, as he shuffled in, I found my impulse to laugh returning, as I pictured him with Miss Potter. He was very deaf, so I couldn't sit down and talk in a confidential tone. The necessity to raise the level of my voice meant that it could not be the kind of private 'ticking off' that would have been more suitable in the circumstances.

I managed to compose myself sufficiently to make certain he understood that his action had insulted Miss Potter. She had been made to feel like a woman of ill repute to be propositioned in that way. Returning his money to him, I suggested that he should find the earliest opportunity to apologise to her for the embarrassment he had caused.

He seemed sorry enough at the time, and made what appeared to be a genuine apology to her. However, he was a game old boy, because other staff were often reporting that he had 'touched them up' when they were confined in the lift with him. In those days it was all taken in good part, for there was little time to think of such things as 'sexual harassment'.

Another member of staff, Gurmeet, who had originally come from overseas, was our newly-appointed Assistant Matron. An Indian by birth, this young lady had lived in England for many years and spoke excellent English. She was a nurse, with some residential experience.

Her family, of whom there were many, also lived in this country. She always wore the long silk trousers which concealed her legs, although in many ways she was quite westernised. The family were Sikhs and her faith and culture meant a lot to her.

One night, after she had worked in the Home for a while, I heard Gurmeet crying in her room, as she was on sleeping-in duty. I knocked to ask if there was anything I could do to help. Apparently she had fallen in love with an English man and wanted to marry him. As well as having had to overcome her own doubts about the wisdom of this, she was meeting considerable opposition from her family. It was customary for marriages to be arranged, and plans had already been made for her to return to India to wed someone who had been chosen as her husband. Torn between the love she had for her family and her religion on the one hand, and the feelings she had for the man with whom she was in love on the other, the poor girl was in a terrible quandary.

The wrangling and heartbreak dragged on for many sad weeks, until eventually her family gave consent to the marriage. Their wedding was one that I shall never forget because Gurmeet and her future husband invited me to be witness at the register office ceremony. This honour posed a puzzle. I was not a close friend, so why had this young couple chosen a mature English lady like myself to play such an important role in their life? I had a strong feeling I was about to find out.

On the day of the wedding I met Gurmeet, Ted, and their guests at the Register Office. Upon arrival I was shown into a large waiting room where they were all gathered. Ted's only relation, his elderly mother, lived a long distance away and was unable to travel, although Gurmeet's family was fully represented. Mother, father, sisters, brothers, aunts, uncles, cousins, nieces, grandparents – all were in attendance resplendent in Indian costume. The gorgeous saris of the ladies and the men's colourful turbans made a bright spectacle in the rather sombre surroundings.

Gurmeet introduced me to various relations, none of whom spoke English apart from her father and one or two others who had a few words between them. Certainly none of them had ever been to an English wedding before, and it was hardly surprising that they seemed thoroughly bewildered.

I was carrying one of those silver horseshoes that brides often receive after the ceremony. Several of the guests kept pointing to it, until Gurmeet asked if I could explain to her and them what it was for. This had to be done mainly by actions rather than words, like a game of charades. Then we were ushered into the room where the couple were to be joined in matrimony.

Gurmeet, Ted, and I sat in the front row. The seats behind us were soon overflowing with everyone else; some having to be content with standing round the edges of the room. The lady who was officiating stood facing us all behind a table tastefully decorated with flowers. After ascertaining that Gurmeet understood she could take only one husband in this country (or at least only one at a time) she proceeded with the necessary formalities.

The guests, not knowing what to do, watched me closely and copied my actions. When I stood up, so did they, and so on. It was like a game of O'Grady. Because their responses were not always immediate, and there was an undercurrent of advice and instructions being offered, the proceedings took on a slightly chaotic air. The lady registrar somehow retained a very dignified manner throughout, as did the other principal participants.

Afterwards we returned to Gurmeet's home where her family made me very welcome with a varied assortment of refreshments. These charming people made it an unforgettable occasion for me as well as the newly-weds. I myself was delighted to see the young couple happily married at last after so much initial opposition.

CHAPTER IV

Many of the residents in George Moore Lodge had been transferred from the old custodial workhouse type of accommodation mentioned previously. Some of them were only in their early sixties at the time, but they had spent most of their adult lives in institutions.

For them, a place like George Moore Lodge was a palace in comparison with what they had been used to. Yet as time went by, I could see room for improvement and began to wonder if I would ever be able to do something about it. Several of those residents provide the most vivid memories I retain of my work in the Home.

Outstanding in many senses, was Freddie, a huge hulk of a man with flat feet in size eleven boots. His head also seemed flat; his chubby face smooth and round like a well-polished apple. He was somewhat retarded mentally and could be childish and at times positively infuriating. Yet his brain had the capacity to absorb and retain historical facts, which he then displayed on suitable – and sometimes unsuitable – occasions. He was an avid, if slow, reader, and spent hours in the local library.

One evening my husband Bernard was returning to the flat when he encountered Freddie on the stairs.

''Ere,' the latter greeted; his opening word in any conversation. 'When did the *Titanic* sink?' Luckily Bernard was able to answer correctly, 1912, and so was given another question.

'But what 'appened to it?'

'It struck an iceberg,' Bernard replied.

Mrs C. In Residence

This was not good enough for Freddie, who pressed on, 'Yes, of course, but why did it 'it an iceberg?'

Since the true answer to that will probably remain one of the mysteries of the sea, Bernard's vague explanation was not very convincing.

But Freddie knew. 'Well the Captain turned left when 'e should 'av turned right, didn't 'e?' he snorted, with a perfectly straight face. And muttering, 'Hm. You don't know much. I fought teachers was supposed to know everythink,' he stomped off to his room.

Most of the local shopkeepers and tradesfolk knew Freddie and how to handle him, although it could be disconcerting for people he met casually in the street, as he frequently accosted complete strangers. We knew him to be gentle and harmless, but this was belied by his sheer size, loud voice and seemingly menacing approach. One of his most lovable traits was his ability to bounce back without malice no matter how much he had been grumbled at.

Freddie did a few jobs around the Home, one of which was distributing the toilet rolls. One afternoon when I was not on duty I decided to stroll round a very high class department store which was nearby.

There I was, minding my own business, enjoying my little break from the Home in this comparatively luxurious setting, when without warning a raucous voice boomed out,

''Ere, Matron! I'll take the toilet rolls round when I get back.'

On the far side of the counter was the considerable figure of Freddie, obviously addressing me. Desperately I tried to make it appear otherwise, as I felt all eyes in the store turned on me. Recovering my composure, and briefly acknowledging to Freddie that I had got his message, lest he repeated it, I found myself thinking,

'That will teach you, Lily Chamberlain, to imagine you can come to relax in pleasant surroundings and not be found out.'

Now whenever I enter a similar store I recall that incident.

If there was one thing that Freddie liked almost as much as reading and talking, it was going to bazaars and jumble sales. He usually returned from these excursions carrying some useless items he had acquired. Because of his earlier life, when he was hardly allowed out unsupervised and had no money to buy anything, the purchase of what others might term 'junk' was a source of real pleasure and satisfaction for him. Trinkets and clothes that others had discarded were treasures in his eyes.

After one such visit to a jumble sale he showed me a rusty metal object, a kind of shoemaker's last on which shoes or boots of varying sizes could be fitted whilst being repaired. The usual name for this implement was a 'hobbing foot.' Freddie used to sit outside the Home repairing his own boots on this foot, looking like an outsize version of the cobbler in 'The Elves and the Shoemaker' fairy tale.

One day he solemnly informed me that he was going to leave his hobbing foot to the Home when he died; and I, entering into the spirit of things, responded that I would have it mounted and placed in the front hall.

On another occasion he found out there was to be a bazaar at Bernard's school, a short distance away from the Home. A surprise was in store for Bernard when Freddie arrived on the scene. And an even greater surprise occurred a little later when someone was asking to be directed to Mr Chamberlain, the Deputy Headmaster. As Bernard, who was serving on one of the stalls, was pointed out, the stentorian tones of Freddie could be heard across the hall,

"Ere. 'E ain't no Deputy 'Eadmaster. 'E lives in the old folks 'ome along o' me.' Collapse of Bernard's pretensions to dignity, reminiscent of my experience in the local department store.

Recollections of Freddie bring to mind memories of Bertie, for in some ways they were a duo whilst remaining distinct individuals. Bertie, too, did odd jobs in the Home. Sometimes he and Freddie were working together, or more usually Bertie was working and Freddie was talking to him.

Mrs C. In Residence

Bertie was a small, slightly built, pale-looking man. He was so quiet that in any conversation, especially with someone as garrulous as Freddie, he was a listener for the most part, hardly ever indulging in contributions himself.

One of his jobs was to prepare the potatoes every evening ready for the next day. He put them through the peeling machine in the kitchen, then dug out their 'eyes'.

Never were the effects of institutionalisation brought home to me so vividly as on one evening when I was preparing some food in the kitchen of the Home. Bertie was occupied with his potato-peeling.

With only the two of us present, I was trying to encourage him to join in a bit of conversation, when suddenly, out of the corner of my eye, I noticed a mouse. It ran across the floor into the corner. Screaming with terror, I jumped up on the table.

'Bertie, Bertie! There's a mouse,' I gasped, pointing to the corner where it had run.

To this day I have never seen such a robot-like response. It seemed to come automatically. Picking up a little shovel which was near him, Bertie walked calmly to the corner, walloped the mouse with the shovel, then picked it up on the shovel, took it outside to the dustbin, returned to the sink, rinsed his hands and carried on doing the potatoes. All this was carried out with no change of expression and in complete silence. It dawned on me that this kind of situation had probably been an everyday occurrence for him when he was in the workhouse. He was programmed to react accordingly.

It is sad to think that perhaps he had been placed in the workhouse merely because he was so unassuming that he was thought to be 'simple'. At the time I am writing about, people were admitted to Homes such as George Moore Lodge without any records of their earlier lives. The current practice of having case histories for residents when they enter Homes may appear to be an unnecessary bureaucratic procedure. However, such information can often be useful in understanding the reasons for a person's behaviour, so making it easier to provide the most appropriate help and support.

It must be obvious that anyone like Bertie, with a naturally quiet disposition would not have become more self-confident in the workhouse type regime, and by the time he came to George Moore Lodge it was too late to do much about it. The staff, therefore, felt bound to make special efforts to ensure that he was not going short of anything or being overlooked, because he would never complain – unlike some of the residents.

Even when he was not well, staff had to tell him, instead of the other way round. He was well-liked, and I personally grew fond of him because he had such a gentle, uncomplaining nature. Bertie was a good example of the residents about whom I now reflect. If they had been born later how different their lives would have been. But that, I suppose, applies to all of us.

Lizzie was another resident who had spent all her life in institutions. Slightly Down's Syndrome, she could be loving and affectionate one minute, sulky and bad-tempered the next. Squat in appearance and of generous physical proportions, she waddled rather than walked.

Every day before meals were to be served Lizzie appeared in the dining room to carry out her job – laying up the tables. Woe betide anyone who touched or shifted anything after she had placed it. Any such interference would cause her amiable if toothy smile to be replaced instantly by a fierce scowl and incoherent mutterings.

Frequently, when in a bad mood, she packed her belongings and threatened to leave the Home. We resorted to all kinds of bribes to persuade her to change her mind. Probably she worked out that her threats to leave had some benefits for her resulting from our attempts to keep her in the Home. It was a form of blackmail she was using very successfully, and we were becoming increasingly desperate in our efforts to counter it. One day I decided to call her bluff, and told her that if she wanted to leave she had better do so.

Lizzie duly packed her bags with her few possessions, waddled out of the front door, and down the drive as far as the gate. Unobserved, I watched her movements from the office. It was a cold, miserable day, not really the sort of weather that one would choose to go out in. For a few minutes she stood at the gate obviously pondering her next move. She shivered slightly and pulled her coat a little tighter. Then she turned and retraced her steps, quickening after she had made her decision, as if afraid that her capitulation might be seen. We never mentioned the incident to her and she never again threatened to leave.

One day I took several residents, including Lizzie, for a ride in the Home's Minibus. We were going to High Beech, I promised, not realising that Lizzie didn't know where High Beech was. It was a beauty spot in Epping Forest, about ten miles from the Home. A popular tourist attraction in the locality, it was often used for pictures depicting beautiful forest scenes. But no picture could have illustrated anything more clearly than Lizzie's feelings were shown by the expression on her face when we reached High Beech.

'Where's the beach?' she demanded, gloomily gazing around. 'I thought you were bringing us to the beach,' she added accusingly, making it appear that I had deliberately set out to mislead her. Naturally I was upset by the misunderstanding, and patiently tried to console her, promising that we would indeed be going to the seaside another day, meanwhile she could enjoy the delightful place she had been brought to. It was all in vain; she refused to listen and promptly retreated into one of her sulky sessions, which this time lasted for days.

Until she eventually recovered from her disappointment, Lizzie refused to speak to me. Yet ironically, when I left the Home at last, to take up a new post, Lizzie was the one who came forward to present me with my leaving gift, plus a great big kiss. Dear Lizzie.

It was disturbing to discover that another resident, Emily, had been confined to institutions all her life solely because she was an epileptic; the more so as she was an intelligent person. At the time she was living in George Moore Lodge the attacks were controlled by drugs, but by then it was too late for her to do anything else with her life. After years in a sheltered, if previously repressive, environment, it is doubtful she could ever have coped with the world outside. There was no policy for rehabilitating people into the community as there is today.

Emily was a lovely lady, kind and gentle. She had appropriated for herself the task of arranging flowers throughout the Home. As well as those brought in by visitors for the residents' bedrooms, there was usually a plentiful supply of sprays and bunches brought in after funerals. It was thought a good idea that any surplus flowers, having served their prime purpose, should cheer the living instead of just being left to wither unseen as might otherwise happen.

Emily sorted and trimmed and placed the flowers in vases and jars, making sure they were watered whilst they lasted. Her efforts provided welcome splashes of colour along the corridors and in the lounges and hallway. In this, as in everything she did, Emily was meticulous. Her very appearance reflected this attitude, as she was always neatly dressed and well groomed.

When visitors came with young children, she would occupy them happily and unobtrusively, whilst the parents chatted to the resident they had come to see. Emily never had visitors of her own. With no family and having had no chance to form real friendships before she came to George Moore Lodge, she was one of those residents for whom the pleasure of someone coming just to see them, was denied.

Yet Emily never complained, although I used to think when I saw her playing with the youngsters, that had things been different they might have been her own grandchildren. She had been deprived of the chance to be a wife and mother, roles which she could have fulfilled perfectly.

One afternoon Emily came into the office for a little chat with me, which she often did. I could always spare time for her even if it meant catching up on my work later. It was pleasant for me to relax for a few minutes as she was such a delightful person who obviously enjoyed these occasions. After she had gone out I remembered something I wanted to tell her while I thought of it. So I left the office and went into the hallway. Emily was sitting down on a chair by the far wall. Perhaps she was feeling a trifle giddy as she sometimes did.

Walking across to her I spoke her name. There was no response. As I gently touched her shoulder I saw that she was motionless. Her face was pallid and had an entirely fixed, but still smiling, expression. In that moment I knew she was dead.

She must have been overcome immediately after leaving the office, sat down and passed away instantly. It was a preferable way to go, rather than suffering beforehand.

My very first reaction was a momentary flash of anger that I could not tell her what I had wanted to say. But it didn't matter now; and this thought was swiftly replaced by a feeling of deep and genuine sorrow, as for a friend. My consolation was that Emily had often told us that she was happier in George Moore Lodge than she had ever been in her whole life.

CHAPTER V

The day's routine at George Moore Lodge started about 6.00 a.m. (similar to hospitals) when the Night Attendants took morning tea to wake the residents. The reason for this early start was that everything was geared to mealtimes which had to take the Cook's working hours into account.

At that time the authorities' expectations were such that it would have been unthinkable for residents not to have a cooked breakfast, which had to be at 8.30 a.m. to allow time for the preparation of lunch at 12 noon, so that high tea could be at 4.00 p.m. before the cook went home. One can imagine what a hectic rush it was for the day staff when they came on duty at 7.30 a.m. getting everyone down for breakfast, especially as many residents required some kind of assistance to get washed and dressed.

Arrangements were much more preferable at Brewster House, the Home I last worked at prior to my retirement. There the residents were allowed to get up whenever they wished, and 'do their own thing' for breakfast, with the help of Care Assistants if required. The building had been designed to afford such facilities; but more about that later.

Arthur or myself, whoever was on duty, would come down before 7.30 to discuss the night's events with the staff before they went off duty. Then we prepared the drugs, served the breakfast and helped wherever necessary. We always checked on those who were ill in bed to ensure they were getting their food and adequate nursing care.

By the time the Clerk, Vera, and the rest of the staff arrived at 9.00 a.m. Arthur and I felt that we had done a day's work already. With such an early beginning to their day, is it any wonder that the residents dozed in a chair afterwards? I often wished I could join them!

Unless there was some specific activity going on, such as a visit by the GP, the hairdresser or chiropodist, or a social event or outing, the residents mostly spent their days just sitting in their armchairs in the lounges, stirring only to go to the toilet or have their meals.

Residents' armchairs were the source of many arguments. A claim would be staked for a certain chair, and heaven help anyone else who sat in it after that. Newcomers who in all innocence sat in someone else's chair, were often treated very unkindly by established residents.

It was interesting to note that those who had been in the Home for a long time, always managed to manoeuvre their chairs for the best view of the TV, without regard for others. Indeed one could nearly always tell who had been in the lounge the longest by the position of the armchairs.

Later in my career, this claiming of one's armchair was a frequent topic of conversation amongst those taking part in training sessions and at staff meetings. My inclination was to point out that one doesn't have to be in a Home for the Elderly to do this, we do it in our own homes and in other situations, too.

Time and again during any group sessions, I have noticed that whenever people leave their seats for refreshments, they automatically reclaim the same chair on returning to their place. Perhaps it gives us a sense of safety and belonging. In fact we can feel quite hostile towards someone who has sat in 'our' chair. If we are honest most of us have experienced this feeling.

Residents in George Moore Lodge were free to go out if they wanted to, but not many were able or had the inclination to do so. There were pleasant grounds surrounding the Home, but even in summer it was either 'too hot' or 'too cold'. It was quite a challenge to encourage some of them to sit out in the garden.

Throughout the day the Attendants would be fully occupied dashing around making beds, seeing to the residents' physical needs, providing refreshments, dealing with household tasks and mending and marking clothes.

The Homes had a clothing budget, and still do for those in need, although at the time to which I am referring there was the expectation that all residents would have their essential clothing provided from the Home's stock. This was such an accepted practice that many residents never thought of buying their own clothes, and families didn't buy for them either.

Mrs Shaw was one such resident whose daughter was always demanding new clothes for her mother, and who adopted a completely unreasonable attitude. Mrs Shaw used to hand the pocket money she received each week from her pension to her daughter. This would not have been so bad if the daughter had occasionally bought mother some clothes out of it.

One day when the daughter came into my office making her usual demands, I confronted her with these facts. Suddenly she went quite berserk, baring her teeth and clawing her hands in the air as she walked towards me. I felt like protecting my neck for fear she was about to sink her teeth into it and suck my blood; she was certainly after it! Pulling myself up to my not inconsiderable 5ft. 6½ in. height, and with no intention of allowing a vampire to get the better of me, I stood my ground. Realising I could not be intimidated she turned and walked towards the door, threatening to report me to the 'Town Hall'.

Unmoved, I suggested she do so, as she was the one in the wrong, taking her mother's money each week, and providing nothing in return. She did not report the matter, but Arthur and I asked our 'boss' at the Town Hall to support us by writing to the daughter. This was done and we had no further problems. After this episode, it was good to see Mrs Shaw with a new dress or cardigan now and again, which we knew had not come from our stock.

The small allocation of cleaning hours in the Home meant that the

Mrs C. In Residence

Attendants frequently had to do the washing up after meals. On the numerous occasions when we were exceptionally short staffed, Arthur or I would help with these or other domestic chores.

Somehow in those early days there was very little time to sit and chat with a resident, unless it was in one's own time. That was probably why we had the impression that we were never off duty, especially as we were living on the premises.

CHAPTER VI

Residents in Homes are allowed to have their own GP attending them, just as they do when living in the community. Often, however, a doctor prefers to hand over an elderly patient to the GP closest in proximity to the Home. Inevitably there is one GP who has most of the residents registered with him.

Each establishment makes its own arrangements with the GPs. In some Homes the doctor will call on a regular day and time each week, and in addition when there is an emergency; others come only when requested. Some Authorities employ a GP as Medical Officer to the Home on a weekly sessional basis.

Many people in charge of Homes claim they have difficulty getting doctors to visit; and when they do, they have very little time and patience with the old folk. Speaking personally, I always found the doctors were very considerate, and gave much of their precious time to the care of the residents.

One of the failings in the past was that residents' drugs were not reviewed frequently enough. This meant that they were sometimes on certain medication for much longer than they should have been. Consequently the drugs were then having no effect at all or causing unexplained side effects. Most GPs are aware of this now, and at Brewster House the drugs were reviewed regularly.

This problem applies not only to residents in a Home; it also happens to people living in the community. We used to have an old gentleman who came into Brewster House for a couple of weeks now and again.

On one occasion he was not his usual self. He was behaving in a very bizarre fashion, wandering round the garden, barking like a dog, even stopping at the trees to cock his leg.

He had to be admitted to hospital. Following some tests it was discovered that he had Mogadon poisoning, through tablets he had been taking to help him to sleep. His GP had just kept writing out the prescription, so that he was on them much longer than he should have been. When the hospital withdrew the Mogadon and his system was cleared of them, he reverted to his normal behaviour. On his next stay with us he was fine.

The doctors write out individual prescriptions for each resident, and in those early days when I was Deputy at George Moore Lodge it was one of my duties to take the prescriptions to the chemist. When they were ready for collection, the pharmacist phoned to let me know, and when I was exceptionally busy, Freddie would go to collect them for me. He viewed this as an honour, and carried out the task with absolute dedication, although the pharmacist was probably driven mad by his constant chatter. It was my responsibility to check that all the drugs were correct and that adequate records were kept of all medication.

Staff working in Social Services Homes are not employed as nurses. Therefore apart from applying small dressings when necessary, and practising tender loving care within the realms of home nursing, staff rely on the Community Nurses, previously District Nurses, to do anything requiring trained skills.

My most vivid recollection of doctors over the years is Dr Knowles, who had most of the George Moore Lodge residents registered with him. He was a kind and understanding man. Tall and well built, his thick mop of grey hair always cascaded in unruly fashion over his forehead.

Many is the time that, having been called up in the night to deal with an emergency, we would sit in the office afterwards, chatting, with a cup of tea to help us recover. We must have looked an odd couple, the doctor unshaven and unwashed, his pyjamas still on under his jacket, whilst my unwashed features were topped by dishevelled hair, as I hugged a dressing gown around my nightdress to keep out the night chill. It was a good thing I didn't have any false teeth in those days, as I do now, for there would surely have been hardly time to put them in, and I dread to think what I would have looked like then.

As mentioned earlier, there was a sick room located on the ground floor of George Moore Lodge. Because of the multiple occupancy of most bedrooms, it was necessary to have somewhere to nurse a resident who was ill, to save disturbing others, and to place deceased residents awaiting removal by the undertaker. Nowadays, with many more single bedrooms becoming available, residents can be nursed in their own rooms, which is much preferable. When we are ill, familiar surroundings are always a comfort for us.

One of the worst night emergencies I ever experienced was at George Moore Lodge. I was called up with a terrible urgency by Miss Potter. This was at the time when there was only one attendant on duty at night. Apparently one of the residents, Mrs Dyke, had quite suddenly gone completely berserk. Having smashed the glass panel on the front door, she had crawled through it, cutting herself to smithereens in the process. By the time I had grabbed a dressing gown and dashed downstairs, she was lying out on the pavement in pools of blood.

Telling Miss Potter to go in and fetch a chair, some blankets and towels, I stayed with Mrs Dyke. She couldn't be left on the pavement as it had been raining. Somehow we managed to lift her on to the chair, wrapped towels around her and covered her with blankets. Then I ran in to phone for an ambulance, and she was duly taken to hospital.

When we had cleaned off the mud and blood in which we were covered, Miss Potter and I tackled the mess in the front hall. Having cleared up the glass, we fixed a large piece of cardboard across the gaping hole in the door. There was then not much more we could do until morning. As usual, a cup of tea helped us to recover from the shock of all that had happened.

After a wash and change of clothing I returned to bed, knowing I was on duty early in the morning and needed some sleep. About a couple of hours later, Miss Potter woke me again. Mrs Dyke, having been stitched up all over, had been brought back. It was unbelievable that the hospital could have returned her to us in such a dreadful condition. I told Miss Potter to make her as comfortable as possible in the sick room, and watch her as much as she could. Hardly a few minutes had passed when I was awakened again by Miss Potter, telling me that Mrs Dyke had torn all her stitches and broken them. She was pouring with blood again.

Once more she had to be taken to hospital. 'This time', I thought to myself, 'they will surely keep her in'. But amazingly she was brought back to us yet again, all stitched up. There was no alternative after that but to stay with her until morning when other arrangements could be made.

Dr Knowles set the wheels in motion and later that day Mrs Dyke was admitted to the local psycho-geriatric hospital, to which we both escorted her in the ambulance. By then the maintenance men had repaired the front door, and no one would have suspected that there had been such a crisis. But Miss Potter and I knew differently.

Afterwards, whenever my thoughts wandered to Mrs Dyke, I wondered why she had smashed through that door. I had a theory. She had been a kind of tramp, scavenging around the streets prior to her admission. During the daytime, when the door was unlocked, she was contented enough because she could get out if she wanted to do so. The shock of finding the door locked at night, when she was craving to roam the streets, caused her to become desperate in her bid to get out.

In those early days, death and the removal of the deceased was treated in a very secretive way. It was deemed desirable to keep such things from the other residents. Therefore, when someone died, very little was said to the others about it, and there would be special arrangements with the undertaker to remove the body through a side or back door whilst the residents were occupied in the dining room having a meal. It was all very hush hush.

How differently these matters were dealt with during the latter part of my career. The subject of death was brought right out into the open, giving the residents the opportunity to talk about their feelings. When someone died the others were allowed to grieve and pay their last respects to their departed friend, if they wished, because the body would be removed out of the front door for all to see. We would also talk to the residents about their dear friends who had passed on, so that they knew we did not just forget people when they died.

My first experience of seeing and touching a dead person was at the tender age of seventeen during the Second World War. At the time I was employed in a factory on war work, having chosen to do that rather than go in the Forces or Land Army. If my family were going to be killed by a bomb, I wanted to be with them!

The local hospital sought volunteer helpers on the wards, as they were so short of nurses. I decided to offer my services for one or two evenings a week after work. That first evening on the ward I was naturally very nervous and apprehensive. Peering through the screens that were placed round one of the beds, the Sister called across to me, 'You, girl. Come here and help me.'

It was only a short walk, but how my legs carried me to her side I shall never know. Looking down at the bed there was no movement to be seen, no sound of breathing. Sister informed me that the old lady had just died and that I was to help her with the laying out. Indicating that I had never done anything like that before, I was told, with a frosty smile, 'Just do everything I tell you, girl.'

When I reached home mother put my dinner in front of me and the full impact of what I had been through loomed large and clear. I started to cry profusely. Mother looked horrified and asked what was the matter. Sobbing and shaking I explained all that had happened. She let me carry on for a while and then said gently, 'But you did it, didn't you?' I must have mumbled 'Yes', for she continued in her quiet, reassuring voice, 'You did it with compassion and respect, didn't you?' Once again I must have mouthed something through my tears to indicate that this was so, although to be honest, I really didn't know what I had felt at the time.

However, mother seemed satisfied. Then with that all-seeing, all-knowing gift that mothers have, she drew me close to her and softly but clearly whispered, 'You should feel proud of yourself tonight, for you have performed a service that we all have to receive one day. Knowing you as I do, it will not be the last of its kind that you will experience during your life.'

Mother was right, of course. But how could I visualise that many years later my memories of that day would enable me to show understanding to others faced with their first similar situation.

My mother's words came flooding back to me when she herself died, a few years ago. Looking down at her poor, lifeless body through my tears, I seemed to hear her saying, 'You did it with compassion and respect, didn't you?' At that moment I prayed that someone else would hear those words, too.

The admission procedure was appalling during my early days at George Moore Lodge. We were never consulted and had no say in the matter at all. When there was a vacancy, someone from the Town Hall phoned to inform us that there would be an admission that day or the next with just the briefest of details. The prospective resident had no preparation either and it was distressing to think that people were put in Homes without being given any opportunity of coming to terms with it.

On the day of admission the resident would be brought in by a Welfare Officer, and that was that. Apart from a few brief details given in writing or verbally by the Welfare Officer, we were left on our own to do the best we could.

One day an old chap burst into tears shortly after being admitted to George Moore Lodge. It tore at my heart to see him crying so much. It transpired that he had fostered the idea that George Moore Lodge would be like the workhouse, and when he discovered it wasn't, he sobbed with relief. According to him, the Welfare lady had promised him it would be pleasant, but he hadn't believed her. So much anxiety could have been avoided if he had been allowed to visit us prior to his admission. He must have suffered untold misery.

An important aspect of residential care should be skilled assessment and admission procedure. Thankfully, many people in Social Work now see the need for this. Many authorities have regular assessment and admission panels, with Officers of residential establishments being fully involved in the whole process.

At Brewster House I used to attend these panel meetings and make visits to assess people in their own homes or in hospital. Prospective residents would be invited to visit the Home, and come on a trial basis if they wished.

After six weeks there was a review when these residents would be given the chance to discuss their experiences in the Home and decide whether to remain permanently. The decision to stay means that the residents have to give up their own home outside, and most of their belongings. These days many of them are able to bring some of their furniture and personal belongings into the Homes, which lessens the trauma a little, but it is not an option they can choose lightly.

What progress has been made since those days when old people were always told what was good for them and had no choice themselves; although unfortunately much of that kind of attitude still prevails.

CHAPTER VII

Outings seem to take on a similar pattern in all Homes. Visits to the seaside, stately homes and gardens, theatres, river boat trips, and countryside tours with a stop at the village pub, make up the usual picture. Over the years it was incumbent upon me to organise many such events and act as escort. Whether it is a day trip or a holiday, with a large coach party it is important to vet the facilities at the destination beforehand.

Toilets should be easily accessible and convenient, especially for those in wheelchairs. Buildings should have few or no steps to negotiate, or alternatively have a lift. Fortunately, these days most places cater for the disabled, but in the early days of my career this was not so, making life extra difficult.

For the escorts accompanying these coach trips, the most time-consuming and exhausting part of the day was what I came to call 'the toilet run'. It takes a long time and much physical effort to get elderly disabled people off a coach, into the toilet and back on the coach again. I have known that particular exercise to take over an hour. Organisers always have to allow for this if the party is to reach its destination on time.

Only once, a few years before retiring, did I entrust holiday arrangements entirely to another officer. He was my deputy and should have been able to cope, but the holiday was a complete disaster. The party arrived at their destination to discover it was miles from anywhere and the facilities were very spartan. There was nowhere interesting to go within easy travelling distance, but nothing much to do if the party stayed put. He had completely failed to apply the cardinal rule of making sure of the suitability of the place as a holiday centre for old people.

The last holiday I vetted before my retirement was to be at a small camp nestling on top of the cliffs with the sea below. 'Could be dangerous' I thought; and warned the party about this before they went, so they were prepared. Only a small thing, but important.

Many unexpected things happen on holidays. At George Moore Lodge some residents had gone to quite a large holiday camp for a week in September. On the second day there was a frantic phone call from the escorts to say that the weather had turned bitterly cold. There was no heating in the chalets and the residents were freezing. When I phoned the camp manager to ask if some heating could be put on, he explained that the whole system was not due on until October. It was unfortunate for our party that such unusual freak conditions had struck in September.

My boss at the Town Hall suggested we should get together as many hot water bottles and blankets as we could and he would personally take them to the camp. Plenty of blankets were available, but not enough hot water bottles. The local shops had sold out because of the sudden drop in temperature.

In the end we managed to find a warehouse that could let us have some and Bernard, who had just arrived home, volunteered to go to fetch them. What a scramble it all was, but we sorted everything out in the end. Once the old folk had their extra blankets and hot water bottles, they had a thoroughly enjoyable holiday.

A universal problem, when organising outings, is that many residents who show initial enthusiasm, often back out on the day. This is exasperating for those who have taken much trouble to arrange an event. You can imagine how disappointing it is when a forty-eight seater coach has been booked and it departs with many seats not occupied. It needs only one or two contrary residents to decide they are not going, for many others to follow suit.

On one occasion the local Rotarians had organised an outing, with four of them using their own cars. It was to be a pleasant drive and a meal in a country pub. Prior to the outing the residents had been given the choice whether or not they wished to be included, and from their response it had been agreed that four cars would be required.

At the last minute, just as the cars were arriving, people started backing out, one by one. A couple of them had had a quarrel about something quite trivial, and that caused them all to be in a bad mood. None of my pleading to their better instincts would make them change their minds. Even when I became quite cross, and told them how ungrateful they were and that it would serve them right if no one did anything for them in future, it still did not move them.

There were only sufficient residents to fill one car. I could willingly have choked the rest for putting me in such an embarrassing position. The Rotarians were very understanding, saying they often had that sort of thing happen and I was not to worry. 'Hmph,' I thought at the time. 'It's alright for them to say that. Before I ever get that selfish and ungrateful I hope someone shoots me.'

Of course, these are really just some of the ups and downs of residential work. Fortunately I am blessed with a good sense of humour which usually stands me in good stead at such times.

Another time one of the old ladies, Edith, was crossing the main road on the sea front, when her knickers fell down to her ankles. Mary, an escort, hurried to her rescue. Unfortunately, the old lady was very paranoid and assumed Mary was trying to harm her so she started bashing her over the head with her handbag. It was one of the funniest sights we had ever seen, and the whole party, residents included, soon became convulsed with laughter. The traffic stopped and people peered out of their car windows not knowing what to make of it all. They probably thought Mary was attacking Edith. It really was a hilarious situation, just the sort of stuff that TV comedies are made of.

By contrast were the tragic incidents. One day, returning home on the coach after an enjoyable day by the sea, one of the residents suddenly collapsed in her seat and died almost instantly. It was a sad end to what had been a very happy day. Although I cannot remember the lady's name now, I still recall thinking to myself at the time how much more preferable it was for her to die whilst she was enjoying herself, rather than sitting in a room with her back to the wall, waiting for death to creep up on her.

On another occasion an old gentleman died whilst on holiday, and that involved much phoning, advising the escorts what action to take, informing the relatives and so on. One has to be prepared for all contingencies.

In two of the Homes I worked in, we managed to raise enough money to purchase a minibus. The advantages of this were tremendous. It was possible to do things in smaller groups according to the mood and the weather. Things done spontaneously are often more enjoyable.

At George Moore Lodge, Arthur and I were the only two covered by insurance and allowed to drive the minibus, having passed the council's own driving test.

One bright, sunny afternoon, staff were helping a group of residents on to the minibus as I climbed up to the driver's seat. A new resident, Mr Brown, looked up at me and asked in horror, 'Are you going to drive us?' When I replied 'Yes', he snapped, 'Well I'm not going in that bloody thing with a woman driver.'

Staff tried to reassure him that I was a good driver who had taken residents out many times. Other residents started shouting at him to get on the bus as he was holding everybody up, so in panic he boarded and sat down. He still looked absolutely petrified and was mumbling all the time, 'Bloody women drivers! What's it coming to?'

It was a very pleasant afternoon driving around the countryside, stopping once to have an ice cream. Back at the Home, Mr Brown was the last to get off. He trotted over to where I was standing. 'What now?'

Mrs C. In Residence

I wondered. To my astonishment he put his hand out to shake mine, declaring as he did so, 'I must apologise to you, my dear. It's been a lovely ride. You are to be congratulated on your driving.' Walking away he turned and winked, adding, 'You can put my name down for all the outings that are going, but only if you're driving.'

How times have changed! In latter years the residents became so used to seeing female staff come to work in their own cars that they never thought of questioning the capability of women drivers. We were an accepted part of the scene.

Nevertheless no matter how capable a driver one is, the unexpected can still happen. Once I was driving a party of residents through the beautiful Epping Forest, with Millie as escort, when a large stone shot up and shattered the windscreen. I had to abandon Millie and the rest of them whilst I found a phone to ask our council transport department to send someone to replace the windscreen. When I returned to the bus Millie had got a sing-along going so that the residents wouldn't start thinking about wanting the toilets, as we were miles from anywhere. Of course, I joined in, and it was not long before the men arrived to fix the screen.

The old folk were fascinated watching how it was done and when we returned to the Home amidst great excitement they told everyone about it. To them it had been a real adventure, and they had thoroughly enjoyed themselves. This was more than Millie and I could say; we had done so much singing we could hardly talk.

Theatre trips could be somewhat chaotic. One evening we took a party to the Victoria Palace in London to see The Black and White Minstrel Show. Our group took up two rows of seats at the side of the theatre.

Annie, a rather strange old lady wearing thick pebble glasses, sat directly in front of me at the end of the row. Suddenly she decided she was not going to look at the stage any more, so she twisted her body round to face me and remained like that for the rest of the performance.

Needless to say, I did my utmost to encourage her to turn round so that she could see the stage, but she refused. 'Don't want to watch it,' was all she would say. I therefore had to spend the entire evening with Annie's somewhat eerie expression staring at me – most off-putting.

Another visit was to the local theatre for a thriller, an evening that produced drama off the stage as well as on it. The first Act passed pretty smoothly, punctuated only by the intermittent rustling of sweet papers, a little coughing (mostly when an important piece of dialogue was being delivered) and the kind of whispered comments we grew used to on these occasions, such as, 'Matron, I want to go to the toilet', to which the standard retort was 'Can't you manage to wait until the interval, dear?'

Naturally we tried to select those who would be unlikely to upset other patrons, but you can't be certain of anything. We were in a row where we were virtually isolated from the rest of the audience – to their relief, no doubt – as the theatre was by no means full. One of our party, Mrs Blake, was in the category of those not likely to distract others from their enjoyment. Thus we were as amazed as everyone else when, at the start of the Second Act, Mrs Blake rose suddenly from her seat, and in a voice that rang round the auditorium demanded, 'Why have you brought me here? I don't know you,' adding, 'Help! Help!' for good measure.

The bemused members of the audience in front of us turned to see what was happening. Momentarily they probably assumed it was part of the play, until they realised it didn't fit in with the plot, and that the actors themselves were equally astonished. Hastily the curtain was drawn and the house lights put on. This had the unfortunate effect of ensuring that we were now the centre of everyone's attention. Mrs Blake continued with her accusations whilst we endeavoured to soothe her. By then the audience must have decided that we really were making an attempt to abduct an old lady.

Eventually Mrs Blake was persuaded to come out to the foyer, where

Mrs C. In Residence

she immediately calmed down. The drama on stage was able to resume. Fortunately the management, to whom I apologised, were very understanding. I've heard of 'stopping the show', but until that evening I always imagined it had a different meaning.

Another memorable episode was provided by our gentle giant, Freddie. At a London theatre to see a variety show, I made sure he was sitting next to me in case of any problems. However, he was so entranced by what was going on, that he even failed to speak for a long time, which was extremely unusual for him. Now and again he nudged me to attract my attention to a spectacular dance routine, or to show his appreciation of some lively singing, and chuckled loudly with the rest of us at the comedians' jokes, whether or not he fully understood them.

It may have been the first time Freddie had seen such a show, as he was not an avid TV watcher. Whatever the reason, when a ventriloquist appeared it was soon apparent that this was something outside Freddie's experience and comprehension. The dummy was dressed as a little old man, and the ventriloquist spent most of the act knocking him about and shutting him in a suitcase.

Freddie was so dismayed that he recovered his power of speech. 'Oh, the poor old feller', he gasped. Desperately he stretched out his hands as if trying to protect the little chap on the stage.

Gently I restrained him. 'Don't upset yourself, Freddie. It's not a real man. It's only a wooden doll,' I whispered. He refused to be convinced. Every time the creature was subjected to a further battering, Freddie expressed his concern with pleas of 'Leave 'im alone. Oh, the poor old feller.'

Far from having a good laugh as I usually do, I was relieved when this ventriloquist's act was over, but Freddie had shown again what a lovable old softy he was.

The money for holidays and outings usually comes from the Homes' Amenities Funds, although residents sometimes contribute. I encouraged them to spend some of their own money, fearing they might lose sight of the realities of life if they didn't. They also appreciated it more when they contributed and tended not to opt out so frequently.

This was brought home to me one day following an outing. One of the old chaps had not wanted the picnic meal we had taken with us, preferring to go off by himself to have fish and chips. For days afterwards he kept grumbling about the cost of that meal. It was actually quite reasonable, but he was so out of touch with prices that no one could convince him he had not been robbed.

In spite of everything, most people find outings very beneficial. All the hard work is worthwhile when you can see that some of the old folk have clearly enjoyed themselves. I have many treasured memories of days out, and wouldn't have missed them for anything.

CHAPTER VIII

While Social Services provide for all the basic needs in a Residential Home, money has to be raised by voluntary effort to pay for extra amenities, such as outings, indoor and outdoor recreational games and equipment, materials for art and craft and many other therapeutic activities.

As stated previously, in two of the Homes in which I worked, we managed to raise sufficient money to purchase a minibus. Considerable efforts had to go into achieving that goal, and it could not have been done without the help of some well-known celebrities. There is no greater incentive to draw a crowd than to have a popular personality performing the opening ceremony, which contributed towards the success of our garden fetes.

Over the years it was our good fortune to obtain the services of some top actresses and entertainers; Irene Handl, Beryl Reid, Bobby Crush and Acker Bilk. It was a great privilege to meet them in person. All gave unstintingly of their time and stayed signing autographs until the end of the fete. It was also fortunate that none of them charged for their services, as some celebrities do.

Bernard's help was always invaluable on these occasions. Even while we were at George Moore Lodge, Arthur used to leave the organising to us. He was a shy sort of man who preferred to be a willing helper in the background.

Some Homes have a League of Friends to raise money for them, but I preferred to enlist the support of the staff, relatives and friends. In latter years, residents participated in all aspects of fund-raising. Somehow the involvement of everyone in the Home seemed to create a sense of purpose and anticipation, and the end financial result was always more exciting when the effort had been our own.

Following these events, I invariably flopped down in a chair thoroughly exhausted, resolving to myself, 'Never again. Why do I bother to do it?' But that was one question that needed no answer.

My personal preference not to have a League of Friends does not detract from the marvellous work that many of them do. Where would hospitals and other establishments be without them, providing much in the way of extra amenities and comforts? Often the most disappointing feature of fund-raising is the lack of support received from relatives and friends of the residents, the very people who are going to benefit. This appears to be common to all Homes in spite of full information of events being supplied and requests for help from relatives being sought.

I once asked the son of one resident, who had never supported an event, if he would be coming to the strawberry tea garden party planned for that week-end. Obviously embarrassed because he had no intention of coming, he didn't know what to reply for a few seconds, then blurted out, 'I don't like strawberries', and turned and walked away. Even I was lost for words, which is saying something; whether he liked strawberries or not was hardly the point!

It was my practice to put up a notice informing relatives and friends of the kinds of things that had been purchased from the amenities fund, thinking that might encourage them to show more interest. One day, when talking to a daughter, I asked if she would be coming to our next event. Her reply was, 'My mother doesn't go on the outings'. This was true enough; her mother was very disabled and refused to go out. But as the notices indicated, money was not only spent on outings. Hadn't she seen, I asked, the special tableware provided for her mother, enabling her to enjoy her meals with a greater degree of independence? The daughter just mumbled some excuse and walked away, choosing not to wonder how these items were purchased.

What does seem strange is that seemingly very caring relatives and friends are often the ones who show no interest in the wider aspects of the Home, requiring these fund-raising events. Help often comes from the most unexpected families.

The late Irene Handl and Beryl Reid came to open fetes at George Moore Lodge, as did Bobby Crush. Acker Bilk came to another Home. Bernard acted as chauffeur for the two ladies as they lived quite a distance away from the Home; Bobby Crush and Acker Bilk lived locally and provided their own transport.

The arrangements were for Irene Handl to be met at her London flat. We would be anxiously awaiting her arrival at George Moore Lodge. When Bernard reached the meeting point near Irene's flat she was standing inconspicuously on the pavement holding a carrier bag. He found her to be a charming, softly spoken lady, not a bit like the bawdy cockney characters she so often portrayed on the screen. She showed genuine interest in his work as a teacher, and told him something about her own life before she became an actress. At the time she visited the Home, she had just written a novel, and its rather unusual setting provided further interesting conversation.

The topic of celebrities opening fetes was also raised. Irene's views were simple and expressed with characteristic directness. She considered that people such as herself depended for their livelihood on the success they achieved as popular public personalities. If that popularity could be used to benefit charitable ventures (such as opening our fete) she felt that the service should be given without payment or not at all.

Many well-known figures from various branches of entertainment, including some connected with sport (which is becoming a part of show business) have a lucrative sideline making personal appearances. Where this is done for some commercial organisation, such cashing in on the fame they have gained in other spheres is understandable. Irene, however, and the other openers we were fortunate to have, felt that the success they had already achieved should not be used to increase their personal income when charitable events were involved.

It was a great thrill when they arrived and Bernard introduced her to me. One of her legs had a bandage around the calf area, and I expressed my concern. Irene explained that she had had a fall the week before and an ulcer had developed. Still she had not let us down. That's the hallmark of a real trouper. From her carrier bag she produced a few of her personal autographed items, suggesting we could raffle them to help the funds. Here I must confess to having kept one of the items myself, a delightful little book, which is treasured to this day. We did, of course, raffle the other items, and I was quite happy to add a contribution for my little book.

Irene gave such a marvellous performance for her opening speech that people were delving into their pockets and purses almost before she had finished. The old folk loved her as she showed so much understanding when talking to them. After her departure at the end of the fete we all agreed she was a super lady who had done us proud. Whenever Bernard and I saw her on stage or TV after that, it was like watching a dear friend.

The same applies for Beryl Reid. Whenever we see her now on TV we recall the day we were fortunate enough to meet her in person. Irene had seemed so different from what we had expected, but with Beryl it was quite the reverse. She was very much the personality we had become accustomed to seeing on TV and in films, and another firm favourite with the residents, many of whom could remember the enjoyment she had given on radio before taking to the screen.

When Beryl came to open our fete it had been arranged that she should travel from her country retreat, Honeypot Cottage, to her London flat where Bernard would call for her. Of all days, on that morning when Bernard was so keen to go, his car decided to show a reluctance to do so, but was eventually persuaded. When he reached Beryl's flat,

Mrs C. In Residence

to be welcomed in for a drink, he expressed apprehension that his car might again refuse to start. Immediately Beryl dismissed any worry by suggesting that her car could be used if necessary, a very impressive vehicle, although she certainly didn't mention that fact. Perhaps Bernard's more modest model sensed that its tantrums could cause it to miss this special occasion, for it started perfectly.

The journey was enlivened by a flow of amusing reminiscences from the lively passenger, considerably enhanced by her ability to switch easily in using tones and accents appropriate to illustrate her stories. Years previously when he had heard Marlene and Monica on the radio, Bernard had never expected to hear them again, sitting beside him in his car, whilst their creator gave a fascinating account of her own early life.

Further entertainment was provided when they stopped twice for refreshments and shopping. An early start and the prospect of a busy afternoon ahead of her had given Beryl an appetite and a reminder that she must buy some provisions for Sunday. At her suggestion they stopped at a riverside pub in East London, where the effect on the regular patrons was amazing for Bernard if not for his companion. Most had gone in for a lunch-time drink, not expecting to be joined by a show-business star attired in a floral dress, honey mink stole and picture hat, as if for a garden party. Obviously delighted to see the popular Beryl Reid, several customers offered to buy her a drink. Politely declining their hospitality, she explained that she was en route to open a fete. Her suggestion that they might care to give a donation for that good cause resulted in Bernard accumulating a collection of coins much more quickly than one usually spends them in a pub. The minibus fund was already richer before the fete itself had even started!

With cheery good wishes ringing in their ears, they resumed their journey. The next stop was a comparatively small but busy market a couple of miles from the Home. The salesgirl at the fruit and vegetable stall recognised her customer instantly. 'You're Beryl Reid, aren't you?'

Mrs C. In Residence

There was a smile and pleasant acknowledgement, and other shoppers and traders joined in a chorus of reciprocated greetings.

By contrast, around the corner, whilst Beryl was looking in a shop window, Bernard overheard the end of a conversation showing that at least one man didn't believe his wife's eyes. 'Don't be so . . . silly. Of course it's not Beryl Reid. Why would she be doing her shopping around here?' By chance the actress turned at that moment as the couple continued on their way, and the woman nudged her husband, 'It is, you know!'

This little episode served to underline one of the more serious matters mentioned to my husband by Miss Reid. Entertainers have their own personal problems, like the rest of us, and more mundane aspects of their lives away from the footlights and television cameras. They may be planning for tomorrow's dinner, as she was doing then; or they may be desperately concerned about a loved one who is old or ill or in need of some special attention.

Because we see these performers putting on an act, we sometimes forget that their own lives may bear little resemblance to the parts they play. While bringing happiness to their audiences, they may sometimes need to be cheered up themselves. Still these thoughts were conveyed to Bernard without even a trace of self-pity, simply as statements of indisputable facts.

Beryl Reid was a charming and cheerful visitor as generous as she was talented. Meeting her was a great privilege. And for Bernard it was one car journey he will never forget.

About the time Bobby Crush came to open our fete he was becoming established as a pianist in the entertainment business, having won a talent competition on TV's 'Opportunity Knocks'. He was a good looking young man, very tall with dark hair and wearing a smart white suit. Thankfully his rapid rise to fame had not gone to his head; he really did seem like the 'boy next door'. Young and old alike fell for his boyish charm and he quickly made himself at home with us. He gave us an autographed copy of the latest record he had made, suggesting it could be raffled for the funds. This was done, and very popular it was, too.

Bernard and I have followed his career over the years with interest, and once saw him in a show at Eastbourne. He is seen less frequently on TV these days because he does variety work and summer shows in the theatre.

The Director of Social Services, Mr Hurst, and his Assistant, Mr Meaker, came to all our special functions and fund-raising events at George Moore Lodge. Often their wives accompanied them and Mr Meaker always brought his young son to the fetes. Mr Hurst would usually introduce the celebrity to the crowd of visitors and residents, on our behalf. Beforehand I primed him with relevant information about each of our openers, obtained from their agents.

Mr Hurst found Beryl Reid particularly fascinating, as we all did, and walked with her as she toured the stalls, signed autographs and chatted with her fans, joining in the fun of the fete. He carried a small cane basket she had brought with her to hold things she bought from the stalls.

Mr Acker Bilk was also just as one expected him to be, although some were disappointed because he was not wearing his famous hat. It was about that time that Acker's record 'Stranger on the Shore' was a big hit. We arranged for it to be played through a loud speaker system as he entered the garden to open the fete. It set the scene for what was to be another pleasant afternoon, and a financially rewarding one, again thanks largely to our visitor.

However, one is not always fortunate enough to obtain the services of a celebrity. I have many letters from well-known personalities such as June Whitfield and Harry Secombe regretting their inability to help us because of other commitments. One day I had a personal phone call from Doris Hare apologising that she could not visit on the date requested. So many show business folk are generous when it comes to helping those less fortunate than themselves, as borne out by the many good works of the Variety Club of Great Britain.

Much of our fund-raising was what might be described as 'low key' which would not have warranted the presence of a celebrity – jumble sales, barbecues, coffee mornings, cheese and wine parties, cream teas in the garden and so forth. All were valuable as little social activities as well as financially useful. Sponsored events were good fun, too.

At Brewster House we had a sponsored knit-in, with residents and staff being sponsored for so much per row. Came the great day and they all sat in a circle, knitting needles and wool at the ready. Agreed rules ensured that all had the same size needles, thickness of wool and cast on the same number of stitches. At the word 'Go', they were to see how many rows they could knit in an hour.

Needles had been clicking away for twenty minutes or so when the community nurse, Sister Hunt, came in to administer a daily injection to one of the residents. Before leaving, she sat down watching the action, thoroughly amused by it all. When she noticed that some old folk's fingers were getting weary, she moved round the circle relieving them one at a time, doing a few rows for each. While all this was going on, I was taking photos of them. Laughingly, Sister Hunt requested, 'Don't take any of me. If Dr Moss sees me in one I'll get the sack, as I should be away on my rounds.'

It was an enjoyable way of raising money, we all agreed on that, especially when the pieces of knitting were inspected afterwards. The various shapes and sizes, with some stitches having been lost along the way and others gained, made a sight to behold and provided a source of amusement as well as cash.

At George Moore Lodge, fun was provided at one of our Christmas bazaars by a male attendant, Les, who had been a professional drag artist. He suggested dressing up and being presented as Lady Somebody or other who had come to open the bazaar. Arthur and I thought it would start the proceedings with a laugh, and that people would soon realise it was a man dressed up. So we agreed to the idea, making sure

Mrs C. In Residence

no one else but Bernard knew about it, so as not to spoil the element of surprise.

Ironically, Arthur and I were the ones to be surprised. We hadn't bargained for the professionalism of Les who played his part so effectively that even the other staff failed to suspect that he was anyone other than Lady Marshall who had kindly consented to come from some fictitious mansion to open our bazaar.

Les spoke so convincingly, appealing for generous support that Arthur and I didn't dare to disillusion the paying customers who had been so unexpectedly deceived. Our supposed Lady was in his element chatting informally to visitors and congratulating the stall holders, his fellow members of staff. Then he pretended to have another engagement and with some suitably upper crust waving of a delicately gloved hand, he joined Bernard who was ostensibly waiting to drive him to the station.

A little later our male attendant appeared, explaining that he had been delayed upstairs bathing an old chap who had been incontinent. Stifling our laughter, Arthur and I continued the harmless deception. It was especially funny when listening to conversations going on around us, as everyone believed they had met a genuine VIP. It had not turned out as we had planned, but no harm had been done, indeed it had proved quite beneficial. Our funds were in a much healthier state thanks to Lady Marshall's pleas.

A sort of sequel to this visit by a Lady who wasn't, occurred at another Home many years later. Then it was my good fortune to meet a bona fide Lord and Lady from a stately home, when they came to open our garden fete. Charming people, they stayed all afternoon, even calling out the raffle draw numbers for us.

But that afternoon served to remind me again of the hilarious occasion at George Moore Lodge when Les had succeeded in adding a touch of class – albeit imitation – to the proceedings.

CHAPTER IX

After eight years at George Moore Lodge I applied for, and was offered a post as Head of a Home that had been built only about three years, and was therefore a much more modern building. It catered for forty-eight residents as opposed to sixty, and was situated in a picturesque county on the outskirts of London.

About that time many changes were taking place. The title Head of Home had replaced Superintendent and Matron, the latter being considered inappropriate for Social Services Homes. Husband and wife appointments were also being phased out.

However the title Head of Home did not last long and was soon replaced by Officer in Charge, although in my opinion Manager would have been more appropriate. Many more officer staff were attending training courses and obtaining social work qualifications. Our role was changing and the term Residential Social Worker came into vogue. Social Services were desperately trying to break away from the old Health and Welfare image, because of its association with past institutional care.

Overtime and sleeping-in payment for senior staff was introduced. Manual staff had always been paid for overtime, with enhancement for night and bank holiday duties. The pay structure was improving and the working week had a further reduction in hours. Many Homes had their manual and officer staff establishment hours increased, so things were beginning to look up.

Unfortunately there was still a long way to go before the myth could be dispelled that staff required few skills other than home nursing and housekeeping. Residential staff themselves were often to blame for this, by their unprofessional practices which did little to enhance the image of residential social work. Some of them would not accept change and some could not cope with it anyway.

No one was more delighted than I was that residential work was beginning to take on a completely new look, and that the pattern of care was changing. For me it was a particularly exciting and challenging time.

Of course, there had been a feeling of mutual sadness when I left George Moore Lodge, but all there understood my need to move on and wished me well, Arthur was pleased about my promotion, and somehow we both knew we would always keep in touch.

The Oak Tree, my new Home, was an attractive two-storey building, spreading over a large area with a car park in front and spacious gardens surrounding the back and sides. Since there were only two floors instead of the three I had been used to, an amusing incident happened to me shortly after I took up my post.

One day I was standing by the lift on the 2nd floor, impatiently pressing a button which I thought would take me up to the 3rd floor. However, nothing happened; the lift doors remained closed. One of the care assistants who had obviously been watching my actions came over to ask, 'Where do you want to go, Mrs Chamberlain?' When I replied 'Up to the next floor,' she burst out laughing. 'You'll have a long wait then; there isn't a next floor.' With an explanation about being 'creatures of habit' I scurried away, chuckling to myself for having been such a fool.

The Oak Tree had been built on similar traditional lines to George Moore Lodge but many improvements had been incorporated. Bedrooms shared by three or four people had been replaced by single and double rooms. There were small, homely lounges situated in various wings. One was designated the smoking lounge, but it just seemed to attract most of the men, which was segregation by choice.

Staff living-in quarters showed a vast improvement, too. Instead of a flat, we had a pleasant, comfortable house at the side of the building, thus affording more privacy than we had previously had. By now Bernard was Headmaster of a Primary School, still in the same London Borough from where we had just moved. However his journey was no great distance, and our son Steven was able to come home quite often, which was something we had taken into consideration before I applied for the post. Thus in personal terms it was a convenient move for us.

When offering me the post, my immediate boss from County Hall, Mrs Turner, had warned that initially there would be some difficulties. Up to that time the Home had become very nursing orientated, and she hoped I would be able to change that approach. Special problems were likely with the Deputy and one of the Assistants who had both done much to foster the Nursing Home image. In addition the Deputy had wanted the Officer in Charge post, which added to the likelihood of my being in for a rough passage.

However, always at my best when faced with a challenge, I was determined they would not get the better of me. Nevertheless, to say there were problems was the understatement of the year, as those two ladies did their utmost to thwart me at every turn. They were quite openly hostile from the moment I set foot in the building.

All the overtures I made towards them failed, as they were resolved not to co-operate with me. One of my specific requests was that they should not go around the building wearing plastic aprons, gloves and masks administering enemas. It made the place look and feel like a miniature hospital. Indeed their obsession with the residents' physical needs was to the detriment of emotional or psychological considerations.

I explained to the GPs my wish to implement a more social work orientated type of care. Obviously they had been in the habit of delegating nursing tasks to the two staff in question. When this practice was discontinued and the community nurse came in when requested, that particular situation was resolved to my satisfaction.

Knowing that the support of the rest of the staff was vital for me, I asked all of them to come in for a special meeting. This afforded me the opportunity to introduce myself properly to everyone, and put forward some of my plans for The Oak Tree, at the same time letting them know how much I would value their ideas and participation. Only good teamwork could help us achieve our goal. After that, regular staff meetings were held, and every time our 'two friends' had done something devious, I brought everything out in the open for discussion. Clearly they neither liked this nor knew how to handle it.

The residents also needed to know about the changes I had in mind, and these were discussed with them at great length. Their quality of life was about to improve, and they looked forward to the proposed changes with eager anticipation, offering many ideas and suggestions themselves.

My two adversaries could not win their little campaign, and, much to my relief, after about six months they both decided to leave.

Many times during this period I had wished myself back in the friendly, familiar surroundings of George Moore Lodge. It had been a difficult start for me and I had begun to feel very frustrated at not being able to get on as I had wished. Thank goodness it was all over!

Following the departure of those two ladies, a new Deputy and Assistant were appointed, and we became a close-knit, happy team. However, the experience of those first six months served to make me realise just how influential staff can be in dictating the type of care that residents receive and did much to foster my involvement with staff training throughout the rest of my career.

At about that time the College where I had done my training asked if I would consider sitting on a working party, as a representative of residential work with the elderly, in the planning of their first CQSW (Certificate of Qualification in Social Work) Course. Apparently they wanted one of their ex-students on the working party and had chosen me, which was very flattering. It was good to have the opportunity to make a real contribution to future training.

In addition the inevitable happened, for thereafter the College used me as one of their CQSW study supervisors for practical placements. The training department of the authorities I worked for also used me and my establishments for the placements of people on various courses. Thus there was hardly ever a time when I was not responsible for some student or other. All this, coupled with the training programmes for my own staff certainly kept me busy. Still it was always rewarding to help staff and students to improve their skills and grow in confidence.

One of the major changes that took place at The Oak Tree was to drop the old 'Matron' image. At my request, everyone addressed me by name, usually as Mrs Chamberlain, except for a few officer staff to whom I was Lilian.

The residents found this difficult at first because they had become so accustomed to using the word 'matron', and thinking of themselves as patients. But as time went by, with gentle reminders now and again, they started using my name.

Soon another change followed, when I decided to abandon the wearing of uniform (overalls) for all officer staff. It was amazing how these two seemingly insignificant changes transformed the Home, and provided the impetus for further changes to come. At my last Home I was so daring that the abolition of overalls was extended to the care staff as well! Somehow a much easier relationship develops between staff and residents when there is no uniform to create a barrier.

Whilst I was at The Oak Tree, regular assessment and admission panels were introduced by that authority. Fortnightly meetings, attended by Officers in Charge, were held at the Divisional Social Services offices. Field Social Workers presented their clients' cases to the panel, so that by general discussion and consensus an agreed plan could be formulated.

This was a great step forward in improving the admission procedure.

Mrs C. In Residence

Out of these meetings came the suggestion that prospective residents should visit the Home prior to admission and that a review procedure should be set up. Oh yes! Things were really beginning to change for the better.

As time went by I developed a very good relationship with the Local and Divisional Social Service teams, and particularly remember one Christmas when a staff party had been planned in the Home. The field social workers volunteered to come in for the evening to look after the residents, so that all our staff could be free to enjoy themselves.

This was much appreciated, but I told them not to hesitate to fetch one of us should they have any problems during the evening. Our party went with a swing, without interruption. Towards the end of the evening I went to offer the social workers some refreshments, and was informed that one of the old ladies had been doubly incontinent, messing everywhere in the room. Not wanting to disturb our party, they had bathed her and cleaned her room. They remarked on how awkward some of the old folk could be and added that the evening had left them with an admiration for the way residential staff coped with such difficult and often unpleasant situations.

I explained that during my training I had spent some time with a field social work team, going out and about visiting clients in their own homes. Therefore I could see some of their problems and reciprocated the admiration for coping in difficult situations. It's good to have an understanding and appreciation of each others' work.

As in all professions, social workers range from the excellent to the dreadful ones. Nevertheless a constant source of irritation to residential staff is the field social worker who, without fail, presents his or her case with the catch phrase, 'She's a sweet old lady, a dear old soul', or 'He's a lovely old man, a real sweetie,' or words to that effect. How often we in residential work found this not to be so. Indeed, would we want every resident to be sweet and lovely? I doubt it!

It is a well-known fact that unless something significant happens in a person's life which causes a change, or there is some physical brain damage, one's personality and character are not likely to alter much in old age. There are exceptions, but generally speaking, people who have been thoughtless and selfish for most of their lives, are not likely to change miraculously on becoming old, and vice versa.

Sometimes, to end training sessions on a jocular note, I would tease the group with, 'It pays to be aware of our personal traits, for they are bound to be emphasised in old age, and we could end up as badly behaved as some of the residents we complain about. Don't say you haven't been warned.' That usually rounded off the proceedings with some good-hearted leg-pulling.

It was at The Oak Tree that I first got into the habit of signing my name as Mrs C. on notices for the staff room, especially when in a hurry. The inevitable happened; soon all the staff were calling me Mrs C. and that stayed with me throughout the rest of my career.

One day, about eighteen months after leaving George Moore Lodge, I had a phone call from Millie to let me know that my funny, lovable old Freddie had died, following a very short illness. She thought I might want to go to his funeral, and she was right. Freddie had a special place in my heart, and the news saddened me very much. It was some comfort to know that he had had a peaceful death and not suffered. Arthur, who had recently retired and lived with his wife in the vicinity, had also been informed. We arranged to meet Millie at the cemetery.

What a sad trio we were, standing by that grave, with so many memories of Freddie and the things he used to say and do. Millie recalled the time she had caught him in the local baker's shop scrounging buns, pretending he didn't have much to eat at the Home. Momentarily speechless, Millie recovered sufficiently to order him out of the shop, explaining to the assistants that she personally served him up double helpings at every meal. They burst out laughing. His sheer size showed he didn't go short of food, but they were so fond of him that they allowed him to con them into giving him buns every day.

Mrs C. In Residence

Arthur remembered the way Freddie used to bounce back after being grumbled at. There was never a trace of malice, he would just start chatting away again as if nothing had happened. No one could be cross with him for long.

My thoughts wandered to his old 'hobbing foot' that he was going to leave to the Home when he died, and my promise to have it mounted and placed in the front hall. That would certainly never happen now. Briefly I had an overwhelming feeling of having let him down, but of course he would have understood it was only our special little way of joking with each other.

Certainly he would be missed at George Moore Lodge. Glancing at Millie I realised she would be the one most affected by his passing. She had known Freddie much longer than we had, having worked in the establishment from the day it opened, when Freddie was one of the first residents to be admitted. She had known and loved him as we all had, but in her case, right through the years up to his death.

Brushing away the tears we could not control, we watched his coffin being lowered into that dark chasm, taking with it so many of our memories. Goodbye, Freddie, Goodbye . . .

CHAPTER X

In residential work, one is bound to be emotionally involved with the residents' lives, sharing their joys, sorrows and frustrations. Many situations encountered at George Moore Lodge helped to broaden my whole range of human experience and stood me in good stead for the rest of my career.

George was a slightly-built man with sharp features and huge staring eyes. He hardly ever spoke a word and just lurked around in corners. Sometimes when sitting in the office at my desk, I would sense a presence from behind. It would be George, his face pressed to the window staring vacantly at me, which was extremely frightening when it first happened.

We knew that prior to his admission he had attempted suicide several times, so there was every possibility that he would try again some time. In an effort to ward off the dreaded event, he was put in a double room so that there would always be someone with him.

One day, Jock, a male attendant, was doing his early morning rounds. As he opened the bedroom door he caught sight of George, poised on the window ledge, ready to throw himself off. He called out and rushed into the room to try to stop him; but too late, he was gone.

Jock came running down the stairs, ashen faced and panting. Quickly I followed on his heels when he gasped out what had happened, calling out on the way to the clerk to phone for an ambulance. We dashed outside the building to where George had fallen. His motionless body was lying in a crumpled heap. He was still breathing, but every bone in his body must have been broken.

We dared not move him, so we covered him with a blanket and awaited the ambulance. Apparently he died just before they reached the hospital. Old George had outwitted us all. He had waited for his room mate to go along to the toilet, so that all would be clear for him to carry out his death wish.

Jock and I had to give evidence at the Coroner's Court a few weeks later, where the verdict was that he had taken his life whilst the balance of his mind was disturbed. Although it may not have made any difference to the end result, he had really needed psychiatric treatment. Sadly, there was very little of that available in those days. Poor George!

Bessie and Ada Brompton (often referred to as the Brompton sisters) were two spinster ladies. Bessie was of medium height, slim and frail-looking. Her hair and clothes were always immaculate, her manners impeccable. She appeared to be a lady of good breeding, very well spoken.

Her sister Ada was completely opposite in every way. Short and stout, she always looked untidy, almost as if by design. Her manner was loud and common, with plenty of swear words highlighting her vocabulary. A cigarette seemed to be dangling permanently from her lips, much to Bessie's disgust.

Whenever Bessie was displeased with her sister, she would quietly remonstrate, 'Ada dear, don't do that, it's so unladylike. Whatever will people think?' Yet although they were so different, the sisters were very close. A special something seemed to bind them. The picture conjured up in my mind was of them being in an 'Upstairs, Downstairs' kind of situation, with Bessie as the lady's maid and Ada as the scullery maid. They had both been 'in service', but would never give any details about it.

The sisters' only visitor was a nephew, a very presentable man in his late thirties. He came regularly every week without fail, and was very good to both of them, but especially Bessie, who must have been his favourite aunt. He paid for their hair dos and frequently bought their clothing. I knew Bessie was special to him, for he delighted in bringing her fragrant perfumes and toiletries and providing as many comforts as possible.

I came to know John very well and it was lovely to see a young man pay so much attention to two old spinster aunts. Obviously he came from an upper class background, was very well spoken, seemed to have plenty of money, was always faultlessly dressed and drove a super sports car.

One day Bessie was taken seriously ill. Dr Knowles said that nothing could be done and that it was just a matter of time. So we nursed her and gave her plenty of tender loving care. John was very concerned and now came every day to sit beside her bed, holding her hand. Poor Ada spent much of her time just sitting in the corner of the room, staring into space. We felt so sorry for her, as John seemed to pay no attention at all to her, being only concerned about her sister.

Bessie's death was imminent when I witnessed the most touching scene of my life. As she drew her last breath, a distraught cry from John pierced the unhappy silence, 'Mother, I'm sorry. Please forgive me.'

Perhaps in her final moment Bessie was conscious of being called mother for the first time in her life. Her lips moved slightly as if in an unspoken reaction, she smiled and was at peace.

At last the significance of their special relationship had been revealed, and somehow I felt I should have known it all along. Like a completed jigsaw, everything had now slotted into place. Later, in a quiet room, John tearfully explained that, many years previously, Bessie had indeed been a lady's maid, and his father who was master of the house had got her into trouble. It had been hushed up, as was the practice in those days, and Bessie was sent away to have the baby. John's father and his wife agreed to bring John up as their own. They would settle a small income on Bessie who would relinquish all claim to her son. Being too destitute to do otherwise, Bessie had accepted the inevitable.

Years later, when John was growing up, his father had had a pang of

Mrs C. In Residence

conscience and disclosed the whole sad story to him. His father had loved Bessie very much, but had had to put family honour before the call of his heart. It was agreed that from then on, John could see Bessie, but they must always assume an aunt and nephew relationship. No one was ever to know that they were really mother and son.

In his grief, John felt so guilty about having denied Bessie as his mother. Still, I hope it was of some comfort to him to pour out his feelings to me. Ada had not worked in the same house as Bessie, but she had been a kitchen maid as I had imagined. Of course, she knew that John was Bessie's son, and her own relationship with him did not have to be denied for they really were aunt and nephew.

Not all the changes in today's society have been for the better, but this is one area where there has been much improvement. People are not so hypocritical or prejudiced about these things as they used to be. How sad to think that John and Bessie, like many others, were victims of the times they lived in.

Some people think that love and romance are the prerogative of the young, but at George Moore Lodge we witnessed a love story proving that theory to be entirely wrong.

Iris was sixty-five, a petite midget. Her face was round and wrinkled yet with a lovely clear complexion and rosy cheeks. Her brown eyes and hair gave her a very doll-like appearance. When she was standing, one had to bend right over to speak to her, and her little legs dangled in space whenever she was sitting in a chair. Most of her life had been spent in institutions, presumably because she was considered to be a freak who needed to be put away. She had no known relatives and had never been married.

Mr Beech, who preferred not to be called by his Christian name, was a seventy-five year old widower, with no children. He was a slightly built man with protruding features and grey hair. He resembled the actor Wilfred Brambell from 'Steptoe and Son', only not as unkempt as old Steptoe, thank goodness.

Mr Beech and Iris struck up a friendship soon after he was admitted, and they could often be seen chatting together. As time passed, they progressed to holding hands. We didn't take much notice of this until one day, when Arthur and I were in the office, there was a tentative tap at the door.

It was opened to reveal an amazing sight. Mr Beech, with Iris close by his side, shuffled in, both with heads bowed. They were like two naughty little schoolchildren who had been sent to the headmaster. Arthur and I looked at each other and for a few seconds we had to stifle the impulse to laugh.

Sensing that they had something important to discuss, we invited them to sit down. Mr Beech then blurted out that he and Iris would like to get engaged to be married, and they requested our permission. Momentarily we were lost for words. Then Arthur recovered sufficiently to explain that our permission was not necessary as they were perfectly entitled to do what they liked with their own lives. However, he was delighted at the news and would do everything possible to help them. We both congratulated them and discussed their plans.

It seemed they would like to be engaged for six months or so before getting married and hoped it would be possible for them to be allocated a little flat of their own, outside in the community. Arthur agreed to approach the appropriate people on their behalf to see what could be done.

My feelings were somewhat apprehensive. It was not that I was against their getting married, but looking at Iris I could not help wondering if she really knew what marriage was all about. Did she understand much about sex? She had reached the age of sixty-five with little or no opportunity for sexual experience, and was so very tiny. How would she cope with it all? I began to feel very concerned for her, as she had been protected for such a long time. How would she manage living outside, fending for herself and looking after an elderly husband?

When Arthur and I were alone again I expressed my concern. He hadn't thought of that aspect (men don't, do they!) but then he too became worried. We decided that Dr Knowles should be consulted as soon as possible. He and I agreed to have a chat with her to find out how much she knew about the 'birds and bees'.

Have you ever tried to explain the facts of life to a sixty-five year-old? It isn't easy, I can tell you. Dr Knowles was very kind and sensitive, initially sounding her out with, 'Do you understand what happens between a man and a woman when they get married and sleep together?' and questions of that sort. When she indicated she knew 'something' it made things a little easier for us to answer her questions. In fact as the conversation progressed, a saucy little glint appeared in her eye and a cheeky grin on her tiny face. There was more to our Iris than we had realised. Far from being nervous or uneasy, she was positively looking forward to the experience.

At that stage we capitulated and wished her every happiness. Dr Knowles did not want to worry her at all, but did convey his concern about her being so small and said that if ever she had any problems she could always come to us. Assuring us she would do so, she trotted off. Not too soon, I might add, because the doctor and I collapsed with laughter at what had been such a ludicrous situation.

So they were considered to be engaged; but as with the young, the course of true love did not run smoothly. Apparently Iris was a Catholic and decided she could not marry Mr Beech unless he agreed to be converted to her faith. Thus began the saga of the on-off engagement ring.

Everything would be fine whilst Mr Beech was considering this important issue. They would be loving and happy together. Often Iris would sit on his lap for a kiss and a cuddle; they seemed oblivious of everyone else. On these occasions, they looked very much like a ventriloquist with his doll.

Then after a time Mr Beech would announce he had made up his mind that he would not become converted to the Catholic faith. A tiff would follow, off would come the ring and Iris would give him the cold shoulder. In desperation he would promise to think about it once more. The engagement ring would go back on and the billing and cooing started all over again. This ritual happened so many times that we used to glance at Iris's finger each morning to check if the engagement was on or off that day. We fervently hoped that Mr Beech would finally make up his mind one way or the other since we didn't know whether we were coming or going with the wedding arrangements. We knew Iris was trying to wear him down to achieve her objective. Unfortunately she was wearing us down at the same time.

During one of their 'ring on' days the funeral occurred of an old chap who had not been in the Home long before he died quite suddenly. As he had no relatives, the Authority made the funeral arrangements. It seemed sad that there would be no family or friends attending his burial, so I decided to go, and Bernard who happened to be on holiday from school agreed to come as well. We had room for two more in our car so we asked if any of the residents wished to come. Iris and Mr Beech offered their services.

It was a funeral that Bernard and I never forgot. The two lovers sat in the back seat, very quietly, but not in deference to the solemnity of the occasion. Bernard could see them in the driving mirror and gave me a nudge. Half turning I could see they were having a lovely snogging session, and now it was obvious why they had volunteered to accompany us.

It was pouring with rain on our arrival at the cemetery. Fortunately we had an umbrella in the car so we gave it to Iris and Mr Beech. Suddenly a van that looked as if it was normally used for making deliveries of furniture or fruit roared through the gates. Our disbelieving eyes had a further shock when the coffin was unloaded by the driver and his mate. It was just a rough wooden box which appeared to have been nailed together with more haste than care.

By now, the clergyman who was officiating had joined us and we

Mrs C. In Residence

followed him to the graveside. What a motley group we must have looked, standing there in the pouring rain. At one stage, Mr Beech, who was holding the umbrella over Iris, began to sway backwards and forwards. Luckily, Bernard grabbed his arm just in time to save him from joining the deceased, and continued to hold him and the umbrella whilst Iris clung on to me. On the return journey Iris and Mr Beech resumed where they had left off in the back seat of the car. The experience by the graveside had not dampened their ardour.

Many times afterwards, Bernard and I reflected what a hilarious yet also sad event it had been. We were shocked by the council's funeral arrangements. The absence of dignity about the van that brought the coffin, the men who carted it out, and above all that pathetic wooden box itself, were features for which we were unprepared, having previously only attended funerals where the deceased was afforded a degree of respect. One would not expect the taxpayers to subsidise a lavish funeral in such circumstances, but it is to be hoped that in these more enlightened days a sensitive approach would be adopted, rather than the kinds of appalling practices which so saddened us that morning. Surely even a pauper can be afforded some elementary consideration at his death.

The sombre mood of that funeral gave way to happier feelings within a few days when Iris rushed into the office one morning. Dan, as we were now allowed to call him, had been defeated at last. He had agreed to be converted to her faith, so the wedding plans could now go ahead. There was a great sigh of relief all round the Home.

Arthur contacted the Housing and Social Work Departments, as promised, and plans were set in motion to allocate the newly weds a flat as soon as possible, and furnish it with basic necessities. Staff also rose to the occasion with gifts of household items they no longer required. It seemed that everyone was having a good turn-out at home for the benefit of Iris and Dan.

By shuffling the bedroom arrangements we were able to provide a double room for them until their flat became available. One of the care assistants made the wedding dress; our cook made the cake and Arthur and I financed the reception which was to be held at George Moore Lodge. Everyone rallied round to help, including the residents who, like the rest of us, were caught up in this unexpected wedding fever.

On the great day itself I must confess there was a lump in my throat when I first caught sight of Iris coming down the stairs in her pretty little white outfit. She really did look lovely and radiated happiness. Glancing round I noticed many members of staff and residents brushing away a tear.

The service was very moving; Iris full of confidence but Dan rather strained and nervous. It must have been difficult for him being so new to Catholicism; but, back at George Moore Lodge he soon relaxed again and they both enjoyed the reception.

I don't think I shall ever forget Iris's face when Dan lifted her up on the chair beside him whilst giving his 'thank you' speech. It was just as if she was saying, 'Look everybody. I've made it. I'm Mrs Beech now.' And she looked at her husband with such deep love, affection and pride. Secretly I prayed that all would go well for them.

In those early days of their marriage they were afforded as much privacy as possible. They seemed happy and contented. About three weeks after their wedding came the sad day for us when they moved out of George Moore Lodge to their little flat. Staff kept in touch and everything worked out agreeably for them. Iris adapted to her new life and managed to cope very well.

It was about eighteen months later, by which time I was at The Oak Tree, that I heard from Millie that Dan had died. Poor Iris, what would she do now, I wondered. It seemed she had made quite a few friends amongst her neighbours and whilst she grieved for Dan, she was determined to manage on her own, with the help of those new-found friends. What admiration we all had for her.

Over the years everyone at George Moore Lodge lost touch, but I have often wondered about her. Was their marriage ever consummated? We shall never know. But they were very happy and content with each other, so what did it matter how they found that happiness? Did she ever have to go back into care again? These are some of the questions that will, I expect, remain unanswered.

What this very emotional and human experience did teach me, was never to underestimate anyone. I had seen love and courage conquer many things, and was proud to have been a part of it.

CHAPTER XI

It was during the early days at The Oak Tree, that I became increasingly concerned about my own elderly parents. We had recently learned that my father had lung cancer, so he was in and out of hospital. My mother's health was not good. She suffered angina, high blood pressure and arthritis. The strain of caring for my father was also taking its toll on her. At one stage her heart was so dodgy that she had to be admitted to hospital, so I was dashing about from one hospital to another visiting them both.

Most of my off duty time was spent in this way or with them in their own home to support them as well as I could. Little did I realise at the time that it marked the beginning of what were to be many stressful years as a carer on a personal level, as opposed to caring for elderly people in my work. Nevertheless, it did help me to appreciate more than ever before the pressures faced by families when caring for elderly relatives, and to empathise with those I encountered during the course of my work.

After I had been about three years at The Oak Tree, father passed away. That was my first experience as an adult of personal loss and grief. I could remember the bewilderment and despair when, as a youngster, my adored grandparents died, and also the deep sorrow when Bernard's parents and elder brother had died. But the pain of losing my father, my own dear Dad, was something quite different . . .

Apart from the initial shock, my grief had to be cast aside for a while. There was so much to do, the responsibility of my work, my mother to be comforted and cared for. It was not until the day of the funeral that I gave way. My tears could not be restrained as the coffin came into view. Then it was my mother's turn to comfort me. She knew I had not had time to grieve and understood my need to let go. We huddled together, drawing solace from each other's closeness, until eventually all my tears were used up.

Following the funeral my mother said she would like to stay on in her own home for as long as possible. We respected her wish and pledged our love and support in helping her to do so.

A few months later I noticed an advertisement for an Officer in Charge post in my previous authority, for a new Home that had just been built, with small group living in mind. This was in line with the current thinking, in getting away from the large group institutional type of care.

This idea appealed to me a great deal, and after discussing it with Bernard I decided to apply for the post. It would be a tremendous challenge to open a new Home, and had the added bonus of being near my mother, so making it easier to care for her. The Oak Tree was running very smoothly by that time; much had been achieved and there was an excellent staff team to carry on the good work.

So once again there were anxious days of waiting after my application had been sent in. Eventually there came an invitation for interview, and to my delight I was offered the post. Mr Hurst, the Director, and Mr Meaker, his Assistant, were very pleased at the prospect of having me back in the borough again, which was most gratifying.

There was an enjoyable party to mark my leaving The Oak Tree, and as always on these occasions there were mixed emotions. The sadness of saying goodbye to so many friends was coupled with anticipation of what lay ahead. So it was good-bye The Oak Tree and hello Warner House!

Now it is one thing to take over a Home that is already functioning, but quite another to walk into a building empty of people, unlived in, and to know that you are the one who must bring it to life.

Warner House was a three storey building, square shaped at the front and U shaped at the back, with car park and garden. The building faced a very busy main road, close to shops and all amenities. It was not particularly attractive from the outside, but the interior had much to commend it, although having said that, as with all new buildings, one could see many faults in the design.

For the first year I spent much of my time dealing with all the teething problems of the new building and its equipment. On three occasions the large commercial washing machine came off its concrete plinth as the washing was spinning – a very frightening experience. Then there were things like electric points in the kitchens having to be resited, doors that had been hung incorrectly and so forth. Sometimes the problems seemed never ending, but they were eventually sorted out and we settled down. Many authorities now consult residential staff when buildings are in the design stage, thus avoiding many pitfalls.

Warner House was designed to accommodate forty-eight residents, and although it was an integrated building it was divided into self-contained units, so that small groups of eight to ten people could live together in a less institutional environment. Each unit consisted of bedrooms (mostly single, just a few double) bathroom, toilets, kitchen and lounge.

On the ground floor was a large kitchen and communal dining room, a spacious lounge for general use, incorporating a shop, which was eventually run very successfully by the WRVS. There were two offices, one for myself, the other for the clerk and senior officers; also medical room, staff room, laundry utility room and huge storage cupboards, which were very useful.

The top floor included a very attractive feature, a fully equipped hairdressing salon. Bernard and I had to forfeit living in a house and go back to a flat again, but it was very comfortable. All the staff accommodation, consisting of two flats (the other being used by officers on sleeping-in duty) and a bed-sit for students, was on the top floor. There was a private entrance to our flat, so it was not necessary to go through the building when off duty, a great advantage.

Initially much of the time was spent interviewing and selecting my staff team; organising rotas and duties; medical and fire procedures; ordering food and cleaning materials, stationery and other items for administration, sorting equipment and so forth. It was a great relief when other staff commenced duty and many of these tasks could be delegated. Then there were staff meetings to discuss the policy and philosophy of the Home, plus training sessions. All this had to take place before any residents could be admitted.

I had two deputies and two assistants. Mr Meaker recognised the enormous responsibility of opening a new establishment such as this and did not want me to have to work to a rota or do sleeping-in duties. He felt I should be free of these constrictions to do my work effectively.

A Day Centre for the disabled elderly was being built, attached to the Home, but separately staffed. When it was in operation a few months later there developed a good relationship between us, and many events and special occasions were eventually shared by all the old folk.

Another Home in the borough, Estra Hall, was closing down and we were to have thirty-nine of their residents. Much of my time was spent talking to them, trying to allay any fears they might have and telling them all about Warner House. It was important to reassure close friends that they would not be parted and a coach brought them to see their new Home prior to their transfer.

They were to be our first residents. Arrangements were made for admissions to be phased over the period of a week, a small group coming each day. Staff knew they were faced with a tremendous challenge, because Estra Hall was a very institutional type of establishment and the residents had become very dependent.

To achieve our objectives at Warner House we had to start the way we meant to go on. So the emphasis would be on encouraging residents to do more for themselves whenever possible. In our training sessions it had been agreed that staff would be kind but firm; consult with residents, give them as much information as possible and explain how we hoped the new pattern of care would be beneficial.

I did warn staff that they would require infinite patience for the first two or three months as there was sure to be a constant theme of 'I didn't have to do that at Estra Hall', and 'At Estra Hall we used to do this or that'. Undoubtedly we would get heartily sick of hearing about Estra Hall, but given time it would fade into the distance.

So the great day came. Our first residents arrived. They sat in the large lounge downstairs to have a cup of tea and a chat before being taken to their units to settle in. If it had not been for the luxurious surroundings they could have been likened to a group of refugees with their meagre belongings in little parcels and bundles all around them.

Many of them were in their eighties and nineties and very disabled. Having been in shared rooms at Estra Hall for many years, they had few personal belongings. At Warner House they would be encouraged to acquire little knick-knacks for their rooms, even small items of furniture if they so desired. Eventually many families helped in this way, making the rooms very homely and individual.

This first week of admissions showed much about the resilience of this particular generation of elderly people. They jostled and joked with each other, quarrelled and argued, vied for the best bedrooms and staked their claim for the most advantageous position in the lounge. It was quite hilarious when much of our time was spent in acting as mediators and referees.

However, it gradually sorted itself out and order came from chaos, but my prediction was correct; within a few weeks we were all wishing we had never heard of Estra Hall. Everything we said or did was criticised or compared with their previous establishment. Staff kept reminding residents that they were at Warner House now and that things were bound to be different; but all to no avail.

Mrs C. In Residence

After a few months I sensed that the staff were about to explode if they heard the mention of Estra Hall once more. My advice was to try to ignore it and just carry on talking to the residents as if they had not heard the dreaded words. Hey presto! Much to everyone's relief this did the trick and within a few more weeks Estra Hall (I cringe even as I write it) was slotted into its rightful place, a memory to be brought out now and again and dusted down.

That was not the only hurdle to be overcome. The next one on the agenda was to tackle the attitude of the relatives. Previously they had been used to having everything being done for their old folk, and were finding it difficult to come to terms with seeing them become more active, pottering about, doing little daily chores such as making a cup of tea or laying a table.

One day the daughter of Nancy came bursting into my office in a terrible state of anxiety. She had gone up to visit her mother and to her horror had discovered Nancy with her friend in the kitchen making some cakes.

'How dare you make my mother do cooking,' she demanded. 'She never had to do things like that at the other place. I thought she was here to be cared for.'

Inviting her to sit down to discuss the matter calmly I asked if she had noticed anyone standing over her mother forcing her to do it. Reluctantly she agreed she had not. Then I asked if her mother had seemed to be enjoying herself. Again with some reluctance, she nodded and mumbled 'Yes.'

When I had explained that we only encouraged residents to do things they were able to do, and there was no question of anyone being forced, it seemed to pacify her. Our aim was to improve the quality of life of the residents, so that they would have things to do and think about. By now, too overcome to speak, she just moved her head in agreement when I posed the question, 'Surely that is preferable to sitting staring at four walls vegetating all day and every day.'

Nancy's daughter was beginning to understand what I was getting at, so I suggested it would have been better for her mother if she had shown some interest in what she was doing. Perhaps if she came again when Nancy was doing some baking, she might have a cup of tea with her and sample one of the cakes! Nancy was a very overweight, disabled lady and the fact that she was making the effort to be more mobile was a tremendous achievement. She needed all the praise and encouragement her daughter could give.

It is strange how small things are often the most rewarding. About eighteen months after this incident, I was walking around the Home late one evening and noticed Nancy in the little kitchen preparing a grapefruit, cutting it into manageable segments. Stopping to have a chat, she told me she was trying to lose weight and was going to put the grapefruit in the fridge overnight ready for her breakfast next morning. This was from a lady who prior to coming to us had had everything done for her. Now she was thinking and doing things for herself. In my weariness at the end of a long, hard day I suddenly felt rejuvenated. It had all been worthwhile!

A greater reward was to follow, when a year later, before I left Warner House, to take up another post, Nancy's daughter came to see me. She thanked me for talking to her that day and said, 'You were right, Mrs Chamberlain. Mother is a new woman and enjoying life again. She has more conversation and it's a pleasure to come to visit her. I can't thank you enough.'

I explained that it had been a team effort, and that much of the credit should go to Nancy herself for the supreme effort she had made to lead a fuller life. It would not have happened if her daughter had not encouraged her. But it was gratifying to be thanked, an all too rare commodity in residential work.

Actually it was following that early traumatic incident with Nancy's daughter that I hit on the idea of inviting all the relatives, by letter, to a special meeting one evening. Staff agreed to come along, too. The idea was that I would explain what we were trying to do at Warner House, and how we hoped it would ultimately lead to an improved life style for their loved ones. The relatives' co-operation would help to achieve these aims. After the introduction they would be invited to ask questions and then feel free to mingle and chat with the staff whilst having some refreshments.

There was a good response to my invitation and the meeting progressed as arranged. I explained that the residents were not expected to get up early in the mornings and be herded like cattle into the main dining room for breakfast as in the past. They could get up when they wished and have breakfast at their leisure in their own unit with the help of care assistants. They had lunch in the main dining room but high tea was sent round to each group.

The residents were encouraged to prepare their own beverages and snacks, lay table, butter bread, wash up and make their own beds. If they could not manage these things alone, care assistants helped them. No one was expected to do the impossible. Sometimes residents shared these tasks within their group, or took it in turns to do a particular chore. Often they would be heard arguing over who was going to do the washing up. All perfectly natural in any family situation.

Residents were beginning to think for themselves; there was more activity and conversation, all of which helps to alleviate the awful boredom and apathy one often finds in institutional establishments. It was also noted that because residents were more active during the day, they did not concentrate on their aches and pains so much, and were sleeping better at night. Certainly the amount of pain-killers and sleeping pills that doctors prescribed had been reduced considerably. One doctor himself remarked about this when comparing the drugs consumed at other Homes he visited. None of the residents' physical needs were neglected, but more emphasis was placed on the psychological and emotional needs of the individual than in the past.

It was clear from their questions that the guests' overriding concern was the question of risk. They were afraid that if the old folk were making a cup of tea they might burn themselves, or they might fall when making their bed, even cut themselves with a knife when buttering bread and so forth.

One daughter queried that if her mother was able to do more for herself, would she be expected to take her home and care for her again? Another said she had always felt guilty about putting her mother in a Home, but somehow this had seemed justified at Estra Hall when her mother had been so dependent. At least she could feel that no harm could come to mother whilst sitting in a chair being waited on, and this had helped to resolve some of her guilt.

There was much nodding in agreement amongst our guests when these sentiments were expressed. But although one could sympathise with them (knowing that because of personal problems many had not had much choice but to place a loved one in care) they could not be allowed to condemn the residents to an empty existence just to placate their own feelings of fear and guilt.

I set about reassuring them that they would not be expected to take relatives home again. As for the question of risk, we either wrap people up in a protective cocoon so that their existence is empty and meaningless or we realise that to live a more normal, worthwhile life acceptable risks must be taken. They should feel less guilty now they could see the dignity and self-respect of their loved ones being restored to them. Surely guilt must be far worse when you have condemned someone you love to a life void of value and self esteem.

The response from everyone was very gratifying, and staff agreed it had been a very valuable exercise. Now we could start putting some of our plans into operation at Warner House, knowing we were more likely to get support. It was an exciting and challenging time for both residents and staff.

CHAPTER XII

My two deputies at Warner House were different in every way, yet they got on remarkably well. Margaret was a very tall, well-built, middle aged, softly spoken Irish lady. Edna, approaching middle age, was medium in height and build, an attractive but rather boisterous cockney character, with a generous heart.

On the whole the staff team was very good, eager to learn and enthusiastic. Some of the manual staff were new to the work, some had been in other Homes, a few had come from Estra Hall when it closed. Although there was a mixture of attitude and experience, one thing was certain. We were all pioneering something that was quite new to residential work with the elderly. Therefore, the constant need to confer and discuss things together helped staff relationships to develop more quickly than they might otherwise have done.

Sitting in my office one morning I overheard two Care Assistants talking as they came downstairs. One remarked, 'I'm pleased with meself this mornin'. All me beds are made and it's only 9 o'clock.'

I recognised Beryl's voice. She had worked in another Home and was obviously finding it difficult to shake off traditional habits. So later on, I engaged her in a seemingly casual conversation.

What did she think about the new pattern of care at Warner House, as opposed to the very institutional establishment that she had worked in previously, I asked her. What were her observations on the residents' response to the changes? How were they coping with the new approach of getting up at their leisure in the mornings, I wondered.

Mrs C. In Residence

Beryl was cagey with her answers. Clearly she had not been implementing the changes and therefore did not know how the residents were reacting to them. At that point I decided to put her out of her misery by telling her about the conversation I had overheard on the stairs, whilst inviting her to think about what she had done that morning.

For a few seconds she looked at me quizzically, then a transformation came over her face as it dawned on her what our conversation was all about.

Admonishing herself, she exclaimed, 'Ain't I daft? Talk about set in me ways.' Then we both had a good laugh and she assured me it would not happen again. Beryl eventually turned out to be one of the best care assistants I ever had.

Small group living certainly has its funny side at times. One day whilst walking past one of the lounges I heard a voice boom out in a very authoritative tone, 'Be quiet all of you. Stop speaking at once!' Then to my amazement, there was complete silence.

Peering round the door, I was greeted with a barrage of voices all speaking at once, and residents who were all pointing to Miss Henley, sitting in the corner. The indignant complaint of everyone else there was 'How dare she tell us to be quiet? This is our home and we can talk if we like.'

I realised what had happened. Miss Henley was a retired schoolmistress. In her days there was no nonsense; children had to behave themselves. Now she was old and becoming senile, so I suppose her mind had wandered back to the classroom. All the others in the room had become her children.

Peace reigned again when I explained this quietly to the group and assured them that Miss Henley did not realise what she had said, so I hoped they would be patient with her. Miss Henley appeared to imagine I was her headmistress, for she seemed to respond to me when I tried to bring her back to reality. Gently I explained that she was sharing the room with grown-up people, not children.

Mrs C. In Residence

Leaving the room I was amused by the fact that Miss Henley had obviously not lost her touch. When she had shouted at the other residents they responded with immediate and total silence. They too, must have been reminded of their days in the classroom.

In another group there were two sisters, Annie and Bessie, neither of whom had ever been married. They were both short, but Annie was as stout as Bessie was thin. They were real cockney characters. Having lived together for years they now shared a double room in the Home.

Annie used to swear like a trouper when she was with other residents and they often complained about it. Bessie, with a look of disgust, would implore, 'Stop swearing Annie.' Not that Annie ever took any notice of her. Bessie liked to make out that she was the goody-goody. But if you were ever passing their room, you would hear her sounding forth with a vocabulary of words that made Annie's seem mild in comparison. They used to have terrible arguments. It was incredible that they had lived together for so many years without coming to blows. Yet if one was ill, the other would not leave her side.

As time went on at Warner House, many VIPs visited, amongst them officials of the DHSS who were monitoring the establishment. They often came to look round and see how the small group living was progressing. This was to help with the forward planning of local authority Homes, as the type of care provided would affect the design and approval of new buildings.

Another VIP was the Royal Danish Minister of Foreign Affairs. She was doing a tour here, and Warner House was on her itinerary. She was a charming person who spoke good English, so we were able to converse without too many problems. A few weeks after this event I received a beautiful, illustrated book, 'Hans Christian Andersen as an artist', sent by the Minister. It had 'The Royal Danish Ministry of Foreign Affairs' inscribed on the front page. Now having pride of place on my bookshelf, it will always remind me of that particular occasion.

One day a group of five government officials from Japan came to visit, with their Japanese interpreter. They asked many questions, but it was a very slow process going through the interpreter, because I was also interested in finding out about the care of the elderly in Japan. So there was much smiling, nodding and gesticulating going on, in order to make ourselves understood. All the time their cameras were clicking away, and every introduction provided another excuse for the cameras to roll.

As we approached the group where Annie and Bessie were based, I gave a silent prayer that they would behave themselves just this once, although I feared my prayer would not be answered as the visitors gravitated towards the sisters for a chat.

Every question that was put to them through the interpreter was answered with their usual succession of swear words. The interpreter's face was a delight to watch, for how could she translate what they were saying into a meaningful answer for her entourage!

At first she thought it was another foreign language, and was completely puzzled until I whispered in her ear that Annie and Bessie were fond of using rude words that did not bear repeating. Then she smiled, recognising the situation, and set about interpreting the answers as best she could, minus the swear words.

How she did it, or what she said, I shall never know, but our visitors looked suitably impressed. Their gentle smiles and sympathetic gestures indicated that they thought Annie and Bessie were two of the sweetest old ladies they had ever met. The interpreter and I smiled at each other knowingly. We had no intention of disillusioning them.

A few weeks later a parcel arrived from our Japanese friends. Enclosed was a beautifully designed fan, a stack of photos that they had taken whilst with us, and a delightful large print of a Japanese scene, ready for framing. There was a letter of thanks for making their visit to Warner House so enjoyable and interesting. Another happy occasion among so many memories.

Most establishments cater for the residents' spiritual and religious

Mrs C. In Residence

needs. Sometimes members of local Churches come into the Homes and conduct a short service of hymns and prayers, or provide transport and escorts enabling some residents to go out to a Church service. Local clergy usually come on a regular basis to take communion for those who wish it. Often the old folk are invited out to various Church activities, especially at Christmas time.

At Warner House one of the vicars from a nearby church, Revd. Ralph Hoskins, adopted our Home as his pet project, and called in quite frequently, sometimes just to have a cup of tea with us in the office. Although every time he popped in he would say, 'Can't stop. Busy today. I don't think I have time for a cuppa,' but invariably he would be sitting there half an hour later, his cup and saucer still resting on his lap.

Ralph was in his early fifties, a slightly built man with greying hair and thick-set features. A bachelor, living with his mother, he was basically a very shy man. Our clerk, Susan, an attractive thirty-eight year old mother of two teenagers, was something of a tease, and used to love to see him blush. When she passed some saucy remark his face would turn brilliant red from the neck up. Then he would give a little cough and chuckle to hide his embarrassment.

He was a very kind man, looked upon by all as a good friend of the Home. We believed that secretly he enjoyed Susan's teasing, knowing it was just a bit of lighthearted fun. It certainly never stopped him from coming in for that cuppa. In a way we felt rather sorry for him, as he was a timid person, very dominated by his mother.

One day, when planning a fancy dress party, we decided to invite Ralph and his mother, knowing he would not feel happy about leaving her at home on her own. Came the night and everyone was resplendent in fancy costume, except Ralph and mother who came in their normal attire. Visitors who had not met him previously were not sure at first whether he was the genuine article or someone dressed up as a clergyman.

Susan came as a saucy maid, with a very short frilly black skirt and black fishnet tights. When bending over she displayed a pair of white frilly knickers, and the full length of her lovely legs. Waving a feather duster on a stick she really did look the part.

Ralph and his mother began the evening by sitting very sedately, sipping sherry and watching all the antics going on around them with a kind of detached interest.

Susan told me she was going to try to get Ralph to dance with her. Smiling, I thought 'You'll be lucky; especially with mother sitting right beside him!' But later, when the party was in full swing, to my utter surprise, there were Ralph and Susan doing the 'hokey-cokey' along with everyone else on the floor. How she had managed it I did not know, but strongly suspected that by then he had drunk a few more sherries than he was used to. Glancing at Mrs Hoskins, I could see that she appeared very perturbed and embarrassed to see her son, a man of the cloth, making such a fool of himself.

Ralph, however, was clearly having a whale of a time, dancing with complete abandon. It was quite hilarious watching the upstairs maid and the vicar doing 'Daisy Daisy' and 'Knees up Mother Brown'. When it was time for the guests to go, Ralph was like an excited child. Probably he had never let down his hair like that before, and I hoped that mother would not give him too hard a time when they reached home.

Next morning, just about coffee time, there was a tentative tap at the office door. As it opened slowly, a very sheepish looking Ralph appeared. Seeing Susan sitting at her desk, his face changed to scarlet. Susan was blushing, too, this time. Obviously the full reality of what she had done the night before was uppermost in her mind, and she was wondering how she had ever had the cheek to lead the vicar astray. Sensing the humour of the situation, I immediately put Ralph at his ease when he started to apologise. Soon we were having another cuppa together as if nothing had happened.

Ralph came in as frequently as ever after that, but Susan never teased him again. The incident had upset her more than Ralph, as she wasn't quite as brave as she had thought she was.

One day I had a bit of fun with her, when, looking out of the window, I exclaimed, 'Good gracious, Ralph's mother is coming up the path. I wonder what she wants.' Susan dashed out of the office and hid in the toilet, reluctant to come out, until I admitted it was just a hoax. Then she had a good laugh about it afterwards.

Whilst on the subject of vicars, I am reminded of another humorous incident that took place, this time at The Oak Tree. Betty, a resident in her late sixties, had dark hair and huge brown eyes that always looked as if they were about to pop out at any minute. Her behaviour was quite bizarre at times. She invariably carried an old teddy bear under one arm, and would often strip herself naked to walk along the corridors. Never knowing what she would do next, we had to keep our eyes on her as much as possible. She would display a wicked grin on her face when caught doing something naughty, and one could not help feeling she derived a great deal of pleasure from trying to shock people, especially the male residents.

One morning when Revd. Brian Hall came to take communion, Betty joined him and some other residents in the room set aside for this purpose. About ten minutes after there was a knock at the office door and Revd. Hall walked in holding the goblet he used for the wine. He had filled it, as there was a large group that day, and he hadn't wanted it to run out whilst each person was taking a sip. With an incredulous expression on his face he announced that Betty, who was the first one to receive the goblet, had just tipped it up and swigged the entire contents.

As he had no more wine for communion, I provided a small bottle. Off he went muttering to himself, 'I'll have to bring more with me next time. Dear, oh dear. This has never happened to me before.' Smiling, I thought to myself, 'No, because you've never come up against the likes of our Betty.'

The sequel, when communion was over and they started to come out of the room, was that Betty, somewhat inebriated, was singing and giggling like a child. She licked her lips and smiled that wicked, mischievous smile when I tried to remonstrate with her. The only thing to do was to get a care assistant to take her to her room to sleep it off. Later, in the staff room, we were more than a little amused at what had been another of those ludicrous situations we were so often called upon to contend with.

Homes are often plied with Harvest Festival goods from churches and schools when they are finished with them. Whilst we always appreciated the kind thought, it was impossible to distribute the items amongst all our residents, as there would never have been sufficient to treat everyone fairly. I used to get the cook to sort out what she could use to benefit all the residents, and then made up a large box of the other items to raffle. In that way money was raised for our amenity fund for the benefit of everyone.

Nevertheless I always felt that there must be many elderly people in the community, struggling to make ends meet, for whom some extra food would have been most welcome. The system adopted at Bernard's school seemed preferable, because it met this need. The goods from his festivals were made up into smaller boxes and delivered to elderly people living in the vicinity of the school. This involved the children, and it was useful for them to do something for others in a practical way.

It was a very successful enterprise, for Bernard involved himself personally by going round with the children to the homes of about thirty people on his list. Good relationships developed between the school and the old folk, who were often invited into the school for concerts, plays and similar events.

As some of the old people died, the list would change from year to year, which saddened Bernard and the children, although even that had its amusing side when, one year, an irate elderly lady burst into the school to complain that she had not received her harvest festival parcel.

Somehow she had been overlooked, and Bernard was suitably apologetic. He did manage to rustle up some bits and pieces for her – and made sure her name was on the list for the next time – so all was forgiven. Another time an old chap came to ask if his new neighbour could be put on the list.

The distribution of little gifts to elderly people, many of whom felt neglected in their own homes, was extended to other times – Christmas, of course, and Easter, when a bunch of daffodils and a visit from a couple of children provided welcome cheer for the old and a lesson in consideration for the young. On one of these visits Bernard had climbed up several floors in a tower block (the lift, as often happened, being out of order) and supervised pairs of children each making a call on an old person.

One lady thanked them profusely for the parcel of food and asked if they could do a favour for her. She needed bread, but couldn't go up and down stairs. So Bernard had to nip down, buy a loaf and then pant up again, with the youngsters in tow all the while. He was reluctant to let them out of his sight because some very strange characters frequented the flats, lurking on the dark stairways and in passages around. This was a little reminder of how helpless and vulnerable some old people are in such a situation, even those who are normally anxious to fend for themselves.

Each year Bernard received many 'thank you' letters, some of which had been written with the feeble scrawl of an arthritic hand or someone with poor sight. Even these letters provided a useful lesson, for some of them, despite their authors' handicaps, provided fine examples of handwriting for the children.

What the old folk had seemed to enjoy even more than the parcels themselves, was being visited by the teacher and children, having a chat and knowing that someone cared about them. Although it would have been much easier for the school to deliver their Harvest Festival goods to a Home and get rid of everything in one go, this arrangement seemed much more rewarding.

The headmaster of the school close by The Oak Tree phoned one day to tell me that the children were doing a project on, 'What it was like in Grandma's day'. He wondered if a few of the residents would like to go into the school, chat with the children and discuss what it was really like in their younger days, answering the children's questions.

It seemed a marvellous idea and when it was put to the residents they, too, were very enthusiastic about it. Elderly folk do love a captive audience when they are reminiscing about the old days. So a group of volunteer residents went into the school one afternoon and were in their element sitting amongst the children. It turned out to be one of the most successful projects the children had ever done, and when it was finished we were invited into the school to view their work.

Most Homes have a good relationship with their local school. Sometimes residents are invited for a concert or a party; at other times, children and teachers come to the Homes. This liaison between young and old is very worthwhile and should always be encouraged.

Recently I visited an elderly aunt who was talking with great love and affection about her twenty-four year old granddaughter. 'She often pops round to see me and we have a good chat.' Then, leaning towards me she lowered her voice as one does when about to divulge a confidence, 'We have always had our little secrets, you know, and I have to promise not to tell her Mum and Dad.'

As I nodded my head in a gesture of understanding, it dawned upon me that over the years I had heard similar statements from many of the residents discussing their grandchildren. Casting my mind back to my own parents and their relationship with my son I recalled that was something quite special, too. They used to share little secrets just as I did with my grandparents.

The significance of Aunt Jessie's remark had not occurred to me before. Thank you Aunt Jess!

CHAPTER XIII

After about a year at Warner House, it became apparent that no matter how much we supported my mother, she would not be able to live on her own for much longer. She had been in and out of hospital a couple of times, as her heart and kidneys were failing. This, coupled with her arthritis, was making her increasingly frail. So Bernard and I had a chat with her to see if she would come to live with us. That way it would be more convenient to care for her, and she would not be on her own.

We gave her time to think about it, knowing how hard it must be to part with one's own home. But she soon made up her mind, deciding to accept our offer. She had been concerned about the strain we had been under, and knew it would be easier if she were with us.

Eventually, after all the upheaval of moving out of her own home, my mother settled in happily and comfortably with us. She was able to join in with many of the residents' activities in the Home, and the staff became very fond of her. She knew that she was part of a loving family and that her independence would be respected. This was a great comfort to her. If ever faced with a similar situation I hope I can be as courageous as my mother was.

Such a heart-rending decision is even more difficult when one is having to consider admission to a residential Home. It is necessary for others to show sensitivity and understanding of old people's feelings in such situations. Sadly, this is often lacking.

Most people as they get older suffer some kind of separation and loss, be it of job, status, home and belongings or death of a loved one. It is always difficult to adjust to these things, and many people never do. The emotional problems of residents in Homes for the Elderly are often related to these kinds of situations. That is why it is so important for staff to make allowances for this when a resident is unhappy or difficult and it seems out of character.

Visiting many geriatric wards and hospitals in the course of my work, I saw much that absolutely appalled me. Patients were sat out on commodes for all to see. False teeth were taken out at the end of the day, as if on a factory conveyor belt. Every person was referred to as 'Gran,' individual identity being denied. All this, added to some personal experiences connected with my own parents, caused me to have many an altercation with some unsuspecting nurse or Ward Sister, about standards of care.

Towards the latter part of my father's life he was blind. When visiting him in hospital one day, I noticed his lunch standing on the bed trolley, cold and greasy. When asked why he had not eaten it, he said he didn't know it was there. No one had told him! Another day I noticed he hadn't been washed. Apparently a nurse had just put a bowl of water by his bed expecting him to wash himself, without helping him to feel where the bowl had been placed. Later she had taken it away without checking whether he had managed to wash or not.

There were always plenty of nurses standing around this ward, chatting to each other. So knowing they could not make the excuse of being short-staffed, I took myself off to the Sister's office and asked her if she had any inkling of what it must be like to be blind, and then proceeded to pour out my complaints.

In conclusion, and before stomping out of her office, I threatened to report the disgusting state of affairs to the local newspaper if the standard of care did not improve. Then just for good measure, my parting shot was, 'Though come to think of it, the national newspapers would be a better bet.'

After that incident, Dad's treatment improved greatly, and the nurses seemed better occupied in caring for the other patients, too. But following Dad's discharge I often wondered if they reverted to their dilatory ways again, and could not help feeling sorry for those patients who had no one to fight for them.

Another time when visiting my mother in the geriatric ward of the local hospital, I noticed she seemed to be very upset about something. Apparently she had been given some rice pudding in a dish at lunchtime. When she had finished it, she noticed a nursery rhyme at the bottom of the dish. The effect of being treated as a child had distressed her considerably. How could anyone be so insensitive, I asked myself?

Having previously observed that what should be hot meals were invariably cold by the time they reached the patients, and now being told about the nursery rhyme motif, I sallied forth to do battle once more. The Sister's reaction showed that she could not see what all the fuss was about, and had no understanding whatsoever about robbing elderly people of their self-esteem. As for the food being cold, 'If the old folk complained, it could always be reheated,' she barked.

Momentarily stunned, I recovered my composure to point out that, as she should know very well, old people are amongst the most vulnerable of patients. Many of them would not complain, even if they could, for fear of provoking some retaliation. As Sister of the ward, she was responsible for the standard of care. This time, she was the one lost for words. She had been hit where it stung.

Needless to say, I didn't allow my mother to remain there and discharged her into my care at Warner House. This happened just prior to her decision to live with us.

Once again I was plagued by the thought that there were so many old folk in hospital being treated with little or no individual respect, with no one to fight their battles for them. It was mainly a question of attitudes towards the elderly, and up to that time geriatrics had not been a very high priority in nurses' training.

To be fair, there have been many improvements in recent years in some hospitals, and much is being done to provide better geriatric care. Even so, some of these incidents referred to happened as recently as 1979, so it is unlikely that there have been more than a few changes in some hospitals and residential homes since then.

A recently retired friend of mine related an episode that happened when she was an Assistant Nursing Officer. One of her duties was to inspect the wards. Entering the geriatric ward one day, she was appalled to see a row of elderly patients sitting on commodes in the middle of the room, with no privacy whatever. Of course, she dealt with the Ward Sister immediately, and reported it to the Senior Nursing Officer. This did not happen back in the dim and distant past, as one might be justified in thinking. It was in 1980 – a sobering thought!

Whilst at Warner House I expressed my concern about the quality of care for old people in many hospitals, relating my observations and experiences to our training section officers. With their help, and the co-operation of the local health authority we embarked on a programme involving student nurses in visiting the Home, spending a day or two observing our approach to the elderly.

Each group was given a little talk on arrival, allowing time for questions and answers at the end of the day. In between time, they worked with care assistants and had the opportunity to talk to residents, whose agreement for this had already been sought.

The sessions soon became very popular, and all the local hospitals included a visit to Warner House on their student nurses' curriculum. Our theme was that of respect for a person's individuality and identity, hence the importance of addressing patients by name; and the fostering of privacy, dignity and self respect, to which everyone has a right, no matter how old they are.

After a while, these sessions were extended to Home Helps and other interested groups. Although it was very time consuming for myself and my staff, doing something positive towards the changing of attitudes gave us much satisfaction.

Mrs C. In Residence

There is a poem, reputedly written by an old lady and found in her bedside locker after she died in hospital. Now frequently quoted and used for training and other purposes, it says it all far better than I could ever hope to do.

The Crabbit Old Woman

What do you see, nurses, what do you see?
Are you thinking when you look at me –
A crabbit old woman, not very wise,
Uncertain of health, with far-away eyes,
Who dribbles her food and makes no reply
When you say in a loud voice,
'I do wish you'd try'.
Who seems not to notice the things that you do,
And forever is losing a stocking or shoe.
Who unresisting or not, lets you do as you will,
With bathing and feeding, the long day to fill.
Is that what you're thinking,
   is that what you see?
Then open your eyes, nurse,
   you're not looking at me.
I'll tell you who I am as I sit here so still,
As I rise at your bidding, as I eat at your will.
I'm a small child of ten with a father and mother,
Brothers and sisters, who love one another;
A young girl of sixteen with wings on her feet,
Dreaming that soon now a lover she'll meet;
A bride soon at twenty – my heart gives a leap,
Remembering the vows that I promised to keep;
At twenty-five now I have young of my own,
Who need me to build a secure happy home;

Mrs C. In Residence

A woman of thirty, my young now grow fast,
Bound to each other with ties that should last;
At forty, my young sons have grown and are gone,
But my man's beside me to see I don't mourn;
At fifty once more babies play around my knee,
Again we know children, my loved one and me.
Dark days are upon me, my husband is dead,
I look at the future, I shudder with dread
For my young are all rearing young of their own.
And I think of the years and
   the love that I've known,
I'm an old woman now and nature is cruel –
'Tis her jest to make old age look like a fool.
The body is crumbled, grace and vigour depart,
There now is a stone where I once had a heart.
But inside this old carcass a young girl still dwells,
And now and again my battered heart swells.
I remember the years, I remember the pain,
And I'm loving and living life over again.
I think of the years all too few – gone too fast,
And accept the stark fact that nothing can last.
So open your eyes, nurses, open and see
Not a crabbit old woman, look closer – see ME.

CHAPTER XIV

Life settled into some kind of pattern at Warner House, with many challenging and stimulating things going on. We encouraged the residents to form their own committee in order to become more involved in decisions affecting their lives. At first we wondered what we had let ourselves in for, with all the arguments and differences of opinion going on at the meetings. Nevertheless it was good to see the old folk asserting themselves at last. Somehow much was achieved, although we never knew quite how!

Group activity had always been a particular interest of mine, and I saw group skills as being an important part of staff training. At Warner House, and indeed throughout the rest of my career, we developed many different kinds of group activities, such as gardening, flower arranging, cookery, discussion and recall, religion, handicraft, art, keep fit, music and movement, music appreciation, bingo, quizzes, dominoes, draughts and so on.

It was important to find out each individual's preference, hoping to accommodate most people with some kind of interesting and enjoyable group activity. This was not an easy task, as the success depends greatly on the calibre of the group workers. It is they who can give most value to old people in a group, encouraging members to participate by taking over some responsibility themselves, thereby helping them to get better acquainted with each other.

All this is very difficult in Homes for the Elderly, as residents are usually there because they have been unable to care for themselves in their own homes. More often than not they are feeble, sometimes confused and incontinent, blind, deaf, severely handicapped with arthritis or having other disabilities. Group participation is a much more arduous task for both worker and resident.

Over the years I have learned to give no credence to the statement, 'You can't teach an old dog new tricks'. I have seen many a person produce very good work in classes such as art and craft, having never done anything like it before in the whole of their life. Their sense of achievement was a joy to behold.

A situation that occurred shortly after my last new Home, Brewster House, was opened, confirms what I have been saying. A group of well-meaning folk from the local community had requested permission to come into the Home every week to run a craft class for the residents. On the face of it, this sounded an agreeable idea. But I did let them know that the residents must be consulted first. They were obviously taken aback by this; the idea of the residents having any right to choose had never occurred to them.

However, when they were approached, the old folk decided to 'have a go', and the weekly class began. It consisted mainly of being given scissors to cut up old stockings and other bits of material, presumably to be used for stuffing things. Whenever members of the class complained, saying they wanted to do something more interesting, they would be told in a very patronising way, 'No dear. You do that for now. It's good for you,' and similar remarks.

This went on for three or four weeks, and the residents never made anything or saw any finished result. Consequently, the numbers in the class started diminishing as many of the old folk refused to attend. They were fed up with being treated like children, and who could blame them for that?

When the people running the group complained to me, I had the unpleasant task of explaining the reason. They seemed to think we should put our foot down and insist that the residents attend. So I continued to explain that whilst we did our best to encourage and motivate the residents, we did not force them to do things against their will. In this instance we could sympathise with their lack of enthusiasm, so there didn't seem much we could do.

Of course I spent a lot of time talking to these folk. It seemed such a pity as they were giving up much of their own time and were really very caring. Unfortunately they had a misguided image of old people, which showed itself in their condescending attitude. They could not understand that our residents were encouraged to retain their individual identities, to speak up for themselves and know their rights. It was difficult for them to see that the residents wanted to be treated as normal human beings, who might also have something to contribute.

The outcome was that they decided not to come any more, and the residents breathed a sigh of relief. However I contacted one of our local colleges and arranged for a craft instructor, experienced at working with elderly people, to come to take a weekly session. I had done this at Warner House and knew it to be successful.

Doris arrived, and what a treasure she was. She had a wonderful down-to-earth approach and treated the residents as equals. They loved her, and from that day the craft class never looked back. They made beautiful soft toys and many other attractive things. She always held their interest and had a marvellous way of coping with their individual disabilities. She knew each and every one by name, and never once did she patronise them. The class was a huge success, proving my point about attitudes and approach.

Apart from this, most other groups were run by the staff, with the help of suitable volunteers. Usually they were just people who called into the Home to offer their services. As their skills improved, many successful group activities developed.

A bonus at Warner House was that it was near to George Moore Lodge, so we were able to borrow their minibus on occasions to take our residents out. This afforded me the opportunity to pop in there for

Mrs C. In Residence

a chat with residents and staff, when collecting the bus. Millie was still working there and we always had a special greeting for each other, often recalling past memories and discussing changes in the philosophy of care.

It was around this time that many existing Homes began to adapt their buildings to implement small group living. George Moore Lodge was one such establishment trying to make these changes, which, to quote Millie, were 'new fangled ideas.' Nevertheless her Officer in Charge indicated that she didn't know what she would do without her. So someone else had discovered what a treasure Millie was.

During those trips to collect the bus, my thoughts often returned to the early days when Arthur and I worked together, especially the day we interviewed a very dapper young man for a Senior Care Assistant's post. How could I have known at that first meeting that he was to play such a significant part in my life?

Barry was in his late twenties, and appeared on the surface to be a very eligible bachelor, although his gentle face and silky skin gave him a rather girlish appearance. Prior to coming to us, Barry had been a hairdresser and a nurse. He was very gifted artistically, and the Home benefited in many ways from his talents. It did not take long for him to become an invaluable member of the care team, and the old folk loved him. But it was noticeable that in the staff room the girls never talked to him in their usual free and easy manner. They seemed unnaturally restrained.

Personally I grew to like him very much and so did Bernard, as he and Barry would often have a little chat when passing on the stairs. In fact, for some reason I couldn't fathom at the time, he seemed to gravitate to us. Sometimes, when chatting together, I would sense a sadness overshadowing his life. Occasionally, just as I thought he was about to confide in me, he would stop short, as if afraid of losing my friendship.

Often when he was going off duty, there would be a young man waiting for him in a car outside, and they would go home together.

Later his friend, Paul, would come and wait for him in the front hall and we would pass a few pleasantries. He, too, was very effeminate, so it didn't take long to confirm my suspicion that they were homosexual. Their conversation and actions were that of a married couple, with Barry playing the wife role and Paul the husband.

At first my emotions ranged from shock to disgust and then revulsion, for the thought of people of the same sex indulging in sexual activity together had always been repugnant to me. I had never felt able to make allowances for such 'goings on'. Yet here I was, fighting like mad within my innermost self to overcome my prejudice and accept them for what they were.

'Barry is still the same person I liked and respected yesterday and the days before that,' I remonstrated with myself. 'He hasn't changed overnight, so why should I feel differently towards him now?'

The reason the staff had felt restrained in his company became clear to me. Obviously they had sensed something different about Barry, and at last my finger was on that missing link.

One day Barry asked to speak to me in private. He indicated that I might have guessed he was homosexual, and in recognition of that fact I asked if he would like to tell me something about his life. It appeared he had been married, but found he could not have normal sexual relations with his wife. Too late he had discovered that he was homosexual. It broke up his marriage, of course, and they were divorced. Then he attempted suicide and it took a long while for him to accept himself for what he was. When his parents found out, they disowned him.

Then Barry met Paul and they decided to live together. He told me that one of the greatest problems they had encountered was the loneliness of their plight. No one (other than homosexuals) ever invited them into their home, or accepted an invitation of theirs. People usually seemed embarrassed and made all sorts of excuses to decline the offer.

Consequently they were deprived of any company outside their own limited circle. Barry couldn't even go home to see his parents, whom he missed very much. Hesitantly he asked if Bernard and I would go round and have a meal with him and Paul one evening. Of course, we accepted. How could we do otherwise?

It was a small terrace house in a very run-down area, but as Barry opened the door and we stepped inside, the transformation was magical. Everything about the decor and furnishings reflected quality and good taste. Barry's artistic talent was everywhere in evidence. His beautiful paintings, sculptures and flower arrangements were displayed in just the right places for maximum effect. The superb, mahogany oval-shaped dining table, with its flimsy lace cloth and delicate bone china, gave the final touch of elegance.

One could not help admire how hard they must have worked to achieve such style and grace. It was as if they had surrounded themselves with beauty to shut out the ugliness and hostility of the world outside. With great pride they showed us around, and I experienced an odd sensation when entering the bedroom. The furnishings included dainty, frilly drapes and curtains. I must confess to a shiver in my spine when looking at the bed. My mind conjured up pictures of all sorts of unmentionable things.

However all that was soon forgotten as the evening wore on. Our hosts provided a delicious meal, lively and intelligent conversation, interspersed with music of the kind we all liked. Bernard and I agreed it had been a most pleasant evening and I was pleased to have modified my views.

Since that experience I have been much more tolerant of homosexuals and lesbians who are that way inclined because of some quirk of nature over which they have no control. It is good for the subject to be aired openly, as it is these days, so that people do not suffer isolation as Barry and Paul did.

Unfortunately, it is now being flaunted so much by the media, that one gets the impression it is quite acceptable for anyone to indulge in such practices. Therefore, the fear is that young people will experiment just because it seems the 'in thing' to do. What effect that will have on their ability to indulge in normal relationships in the future, only time will tell.

Having lost contact with Barry over the years, I have thought a lot about him recently in the light of this terrible 'AIDs' scare. He couldn't help the way he was, and I do hope his parents eventually found it in their hearts to accept him. Bernard and I could provide no real substitute for their love and understanding.

CHAPTER XV

By 1981 much had been achieved at Warner House, and I was restless for another challenge. One day an exciting advertisement caught my eye, for a post with the same authority that had employed me previously, at The Oak Tree. What a pleasant surprise!

An Officer in Charge was needed for a new Home nearing completion, catering for forty-eight residents. It was a new concept, designed as separate bungalow units, with each one housing eight residents. Having already put into practice much of the philosophy for the new establishment, and attracted by the opportunities that bungalow units would provide, how could I resist the temptation to apply?

Once again I subjected myself to anxious days of waiting between filling in the application form, being called for interview and ultimately being offered the post. It was especially gratifying to know that I was being entrusted with this lovely new Home, and that the authority welcomed my return.

Of course, there was the inevitable sadness to be faced when the time came for my departure from Warner House. Being the first new establishment I had opened, it held a special place in my heart. Part of me seemed to be entrenched there. But I knew I must concentrate on looking towards new horizons.

Eventually the time came, and a very memorable farewell party was held in my honour. The Director and many colleagues and friends came to wish me well; but as always on these occasions, it was a great wrench having to say 'good-bye'.

About this time another significant change was taking place in Social Services Homes. The authorities decided it was no longer necessary for any staff to live on the premises. One of the Officers was rostered to be on duty, including sleeping-in, and that was deemed to be adequate supervisory cover.

There was a gradual phasing out of the emolument system, whereby Officers living-in had a certain amount deducted from their salary for board and lodging. Staff are now expected to provide their own accommodation. Those still living in previously provided accommodation have to pay rent and be responsible for the payment of all services they use, including food, just as other people do. The good thing about this change is that staff can get away from their work when they are off duty and live a normal existence, thus avoiding the old pitfall of becoming institutionalised themselves.

Personally I welcomed this change when taking up my new post, as did my family. We managed to rent a small flat, quite close to the Home which was convenient for keeping an eye on my mother, as she was getting very frail and needing more care. We had also bought a bungalow in Essex in preparation for our eventual retirement, and were able to go there for a welcome change whenever I was off duty for a few days.

With all these arrangements settled I was now ready to tackle the enormous task ahead of me at Brewster House. Initially I was based at County Hall and at our Divisional Social Services Office, as building work was still going on at the Home. There was much to be done in the way of preparation, such as sifting through dozens of application forms, interviewing and appointing officer and manual staff.

My deputy, Joan, was the first to commence duty, and with the help of Mrs Turner, our boss at County Hall, we set about getting a good staff team together. Joan was in her mid twenties, married, refreshingly attractive with lovely blue eyes and rosy cheeks. She had a warm, friendly personality. She was well qualified for the post, and although small in stature she commanded the sort of respect that is rare in one so young. We hit it off straight away and our partnership developed into a very close and happy one.

Together we planned rotas, work schedules, philosophy and procedures in preparation for the new establishment's opening. With the assistance of our training section and Mrs Turner, we were involved with the planning of three weeks' training which was to take place in the Home for all the staff, prior to the admission of any residents.

So at last the great day came when we were able to get into the building and start on the 'nitty gritty'. My previous experience of the work involved and the organisation required in starting a new establishment now stood me in good stead. Although there were quite a few teething problems with the building and equipment, thankfully they were not as extensive as those I had encountered at Warner House.

Just before I took up this appointment, the authority had decided to employ a Bursar in each of their Homes for the Elderly, and Brewster House was among the first to benefit from this newly created post. It meant that Officers could spend more time on good professional social work practice, and not have to worry about domestic issues.

So for the first time in all my years of working in Homes, I did not have to order food and cleaning materials, plan menus and concern myself with the duties of domestics and cooks. Of course, the Bursar was responsible to me, and we frequently consulted together, as good food and kitchen hygiene were of paramount importance. But it was great to be relieved of worrying about whether or not the toilet rolls had been delivered.

In those early days it was particularly helpful to have someone else responsible for drawing up the inventory, in order to monitor and locate all the equipment on the premises, but although it was a very valuable post, there was one important drawback. The authority had craftily appointed a Bursar in place of, instead of in addition to, another Assistant Officer. This made it very difficult to cover the seven days a week rota and sleeping-in duties, especially when someone was off sick, on a course or on leave. We seemed to be constantly having to juggle around with the rotas and double up on extra shifts.

The Bursar's post was a five day week one, with no sleeping-in duties. Also, as their role was somewhat different from ours, they obviously could not be left in charge of the premises. Many Officers in Charge of the existing Homes were very reluctant to forfeit one of their Officers for a Bursar when a vacancy occurred, and this was understandable.

As ours was a new Home, we had no choice in the matter, and although I was delighted to have a Bursar it did make life very difficult with only four of us on the Officer team. Homes do need Bursars, but the post should be an extra one and not in place of an existing member of staff.

Bill, our handyman-gardener, the only male on the staff at that time, was a family man in his early fifties. He soon took us all under his wing. Before long it was, 'Bill, can you do this?' or 'Bill, can you do that?'

By the end of the day he must often have wished he could change his name. He was that rare person who seemed able to tackle any job he was confronted with – a treasure indeed! It didn't take the old folk long to catch the 'Bill, can you do this?' syndrome either. It seemed there was always someone going around looking for, or calling out for Bill. It was a fortunate day for all of us when he was appointed. In time, I counted him among the most indispensable of the staff, and a good friend.

Brewster House was a very attractive building, consisting of seven separate bungalow units, linked by paths under a covered way. Three of the units faced on to the front forecourt, and the others were at the back interwoven with gardens.

The middle bungalow at the front was the main entrance. It housed the offices, staff room, sleeping-in room for the duty officer, main kitchen and laundry, sewing/linen room, store cupboards and a large room for social activities.

Each of the other six bungalows catered for eight residents. They had a large open-plan lounge and kitchen; another smaller separate lounge and eight single bedrooms (two of the bungalows had a double room). There was also a bathroom, two toilets, small domestic laundry room and store cupboards.

At first it was a strange feeling not to be in an integrated building, but it was a great asset to be on ground level without stairs or a lift to worry about. We all became acclimatised to our surroundings quite quickly, especially when testing the 'bleep' alarm system that residents would use to summon our help.

There was many a laugh when we were trying to get used to all this sophisticated equipment. A member of staff would play the role of an old lady requesting to be helped to the toilet, but by the time the person on the other end discovered which room the cry for help was coming from, had it been a real life situation, it would have been too late for the poor unfortunate resident. However, as with all things, practice makes perfect, and it did not take us long to become quite proficient and confident.

Using some of the preparation time before admissions began, I produced a booklet that could be given to each prospective resident on their first visit to the Home. The intention was to give information and answer many of their queries. It described what Brewster House had to offer: what they could expect of the staff and what would be expected of them. The emphasis was very much on protecting their privacy, dignity, self respect and their rights as individuals. It also explained the philosophy of encouraging independence, rather than relying on dependence.

Working out the details one day at home, I happened to glance up at my dear Mum. Who better to help me, I thought, than she, an elderly person herself. 'Mum, if you were having to consider going into a Home, what sort of things would worry you, what kind of things would you want to know?' I asked.

She was delighted to make some suggestions which contributed greatly to the contents of the booklet. Just as she was finishing, she exclaimed, 'Oh, by the way, don't forget to let me know how I would get my daily newspaper. That would be very important for me. I'd hate to be without my paper.'

We both laughed, but it was a valid point; one that I might easily have overlooked. So into the booklet it went.

At last, with our three weeks training behind us, we were ready for the first admissions, longing for the place to come alive and feel 'lived in'. There is something unreal about a new establishment with no old folk on the premises. It seems unnaturally clean and clinical.

Many staff who were quite new to the work often asked during this period, 'Will Brewster House ever feel lived in?'

With a knowing grin, I would answer, 'Ask me that same question in a month from now when you are clearing up cigarette ends that are burning into the carpets, tripping over handbags and knitting needles lying on the floor, stepping around walking frames, pushing wheelchairs and doing a thousand and one other things associated with caring for elderly people.'

CHAPTER XVI

Thus we sallied forth at Brewster House, working very positively towards what was considered to be good practice. On the question of residents' rights, however, let me make it clear from the start that everything was not always harmonious. It would have been quite unnatural if it had been. One cannot encourage people to retain their own personality and identity, and then expect them to conform to everyone else.

It is inevitable that there will be differences of opinions, arguments and quarrels, but this is what life is all about; these things happen in all groups and family situations. The staff learned to use their skilled judgement and intervened only when they knew it would be irresponsible not to do so.

The old folk were allowed to get up at what time they liked in the mornings, and they exercised this choice to fit in with their normal habits as individuals. Here, of course, the bungalow units afforded people more privacy and choice. Staff always made a point of knocking on residents' bedroom doors to be invited in before entering.

I could not help comparing it with my earlier days at George Moore Lodge and The Oak Tree, where residents were hurried and harassed to get up early to be in the communal dining room for breakfast. When time is of the essence is it any wonder that the days often started fraught with pain and anguish, frayed tempers and irritability.

Many people said to me, 'If you allow residents to get up at what time they like, surely they will want to stay in bed all day.' I can honestly say we never had that problem. Human nature being what it is, we always tend to want something more when it is denied us; therefore when that something is easily available, we tend not to crave for it. I often cited the example that when we have to get up early for work, we want to stay in bed; but when we do have the opportunity to stay there, we often want to get up. Nowt so strange as folk!

All residents were given a key to their bedroom door. Here again, many people said, 'If you let residents have keys, they will always be losing them. There will be terrible problems; it will be more trouble than it is worth.'

Once again I had to say that it was not so. We had very few problems with keys, the reason, in my opinion, being two-fold. All their lives the old folk had a key to their door; that key represented security and privacy. With each one of us, our door key is usually one of our most treasured possessions. Residents were delighted to be given a key to their door, and whether they used it or not they were happy to have it in their possession. Even confused residents seemed able to appreciate that they had a familiar and treasured object and we never had any of the problems with keys that had been predicted.

Our old folk at Brewster House went through their days quite normally and naturally, thinking and doing as much for themselves as they were able within the limits of their disabilities. We did not do everything for them. We encouraged and enabled them to do as much as possible for themselves and for each other.

It was interesting to note that as the bungalows became established, each group developed its own life style. Consequently there were not two bungalows alike; each seemed to have its own atmosphere. If any member of staff had been guided blindfold into a bungalow, they would have been able to say which one it was.

The residents prepared breakfast themselves, with or without the help of staff as they chose. Lunch was cooked in our main kitchen and taken to the bungalows in heated trolleys; so, too, was the tea. All meals were consumed in the residents' own bungalows, except on special festive occasions, such as parties, when everyone came to the main recreation room.

Residents could prepare their own meals or snacks if they wished, in the bungalows' kitchens, and make their own drinks whenever they wanted. There was much more freedom of choice, and in time many interesting developments took place. Residents were on the minimum of drugs (as had happened at Warner House), probably because they had other things to think about instead of dwelling on their aches and pains all the time. Their days were more active, so they tended to sleep better at night without medication. Also, we did not turn to drugs to solve every problem that arose through residents asserting their own personality and individuality.

It was particularly noticeable that the old folk took more interest in their appearance and there was much more conversation than one usually finds in a Home; they seemed to have plenty of things to talk about. Knowing their rights (which we had fostered) they were verbally active at meetings, and much better able to contribute and make their own suggestions and decisions.

Somehow the residents seemed to take more pride and interest in the Home and the garden. The whole place meant more to them as individuals, than 'Homes' usually do. They participated much more in fund-raising events and group projects, of which there were many at Brewster House. Many of them used the phone to make their own appointments with the hairdresser, or to order a taxi to take them shopping and so on. Staff would take them in wheelchairs, if necessary. Some residents even made their own appointments to go to the doctor's surgery; and some were responsible for their own medication.

There was greater interest in the wider aspects of the community, and such matters as world news. This was borne out at the 1983 General Election. None of our residents considered having postal votes; they all wanted to go to the Village Hall to vote in person, so there was a steady stream of wheelchairs, walking aids and cars as they went back and forth throughout the day, with a great sense of excitement and achievement in evidence.

Another example of this interest was when the residents decided to write to the Council to complain about the state of the roads and pavements in the village. They suggested this themselves, drafted the letter, and all signed a petition. A man from the Council came to discuss the situation and eventually the roads and pavements were patched up. The Highways Department had obviously recognised they were up against a formidable adversary when faced with the collective voice of our Senior Citizens!

Our residents were also less deterred by bad weather if they wanted to go out somewhere. One winter it was snowing when they were all due to come to the recreation room for a meeting. Staff asked if it should be postponed because of the old folk having to come across in the snow.

I told them to go to the bungalows and ask the residents what they wanted to do; and, to our surprise, none of them wanted to have the meeting postponed. They all put on their coats and came. It was quite amazing to see frail, elderly people with all sorts of disabilities, some in wheelchairs, others with walking aids, coming across snowy paths to attend a meeting. We decided there and then that it could only be the philosophy of the Home that enabled a situation such as this to take place.

One of our residents, Gertie, who was quite disabled herself, heard via her Church meeting about an elderly couple living in the village who were in ill health and having great difficulty in managing. So Gertie went to their house to befriend them, and whilst there, shuffled off to their kitchen to make them a cup of tea. When leaving, she gave them the Home's phone number, and told them to ring her if they needed any more help.

When this incident came to my attention, I thought to myself, 'Well done, Gertie; it's good to know that a resident in a Home can also serve people in the community, and be a part of it. Where are all the sceptics now, eh?'

None of this would have happened, of course, if it were not for the very positive attitude of the staff, which was developed through a three months' induction programme, regular training, individual and group supervision, meetings and good liaison. Everyone worked to a planned contract of aims and objectives with each resident; and these programmes were regularly reviewed as situations with the elderly are constantly changing.

Violet was a retired nursing sister, badly crippled with arthritis, wearing a special raised boot because one leg was shorter than the other. Whilst planning her programme shortly after she was admitted, she said she would always require some assistance to lace up that boot; she could not manage it herself. So it was agreed that the staff would help her.

About six months later when we were reviewing her programme, Violet said to me, 'Oh, by the way, I can do up my own boot now; I don't require any help, so you can scrub that out.' With great pride she watched me alter the contract, and we were both chuffed she had made such good progress.

Care assistants became fully involved with admission procedure, care plans, residents' meetings, reviews and so on. Everything was done by negotiation and consultation with each resident. Group work skills were also seen to be very important and much discussion took place on the management of groups. Staff/resident relationships were more mutual partnerships than a 'them' and 'us' kind of situation.

Our philosophy worked because we believed in it and the staff supported each other as a team. One of our greatest joys was to see the change in a resident like Molly, who was deaf, blind, and a chronic bronchitic, coming to us after spending many years being treated as an imbecile, in a very old, custodial, institutional establishment. She started to look after her own room, with assistance doing her own washing and ironing, going shopping with staff to buy her Sunday best hat for Church, attending a weekly club for the blind – and loved every minute of it.

This was all a far cry from my early days in residential work. So many changes had taken place over the years. I often wondered what Arthur would have thought of it all now, and resolved to visit him one day 'up North' where he and his wife had moved.

A further progression at Brewster House was the development of a Key Worker system (goodness knows what Arthur would have thought of that!) The idea was that each resident would have a member of staff who would be special to them in every way, a key person with whom they could build a close relationship, and who would ensure that their individual needs were catered for. So we worked out a system whereby every care assistant was a key worker to so many individual residents; and each officer was key worker for certain bungalows, caring for the group as a whole.

However, it was understood that all staff on duty would be responsible for the general day to day care of all residents, so that no one would be neglected when their key worker was not on duty. But as the key worker/resident relationship was something quite special, it gave residents the best of both worlds.

Our key worker system was very successful and many staff from other Homes throughout the County, including Officers in Charge, came to spend a day or two with us to observe our methods in order to introduce a similar system into their own Homes. Once again I found myself involved in all sorts of training sessions, including visiting other Homes to talk to staff and help them overcome the problems they were encountering, introducing small group living.

Although I had not put myself on the officer rota at Brewster House, I frequently did sleeping-in duty when another officer was off sick, on holiday or on a course. This meant I worked longer hours than anyone else, being committed to so many things during the day. It never seemed appropriate to take my allotted time off; a problem frequently experienced by Officers in Charge.

After about eighteen months, Joan, my deputy, obtained a relief Officer in Charge post within the County. I was very pleased for her as she deserved her promotion, although after we had worked so well together, I knew she would be sorely missed.

I had to start all over again to train a new deputy, a young man called Richard, but it was a disastrous appointment and didn't last long. My next, and last, deputy, Phillip, turned out to be very good indeed. He was married, in his early thirties, tall and well-built with dark hair and deep brown eyes. Having previously worked in a children's Home, he had a lot to learn about caring for the elderly, but he took to it as a duck takes to water. I was very pleased with his progress. He had a kind, understanding approach to the old folk and was popular with the staff.

Months later, casting our minds back to his early days in the post, we often laughed about the time he had walked into one of the bungalows when some residents were creating havoc. Back in the office he had a look of amusement tinged with bewilderment when he blurted out, 'I've been used to disturbed and deviant children, but I never realised old people could be as bad. I thought I had left all that behind me.'

It had been a salutary lesson for him to realise that not all old folk are sweetness and light; just as it had been for me in those early days at George Moore Lodge when rebuffed by the men in the lounge.

CHAPTER XVII

It was about this time that my mother's health was causing me great concern. It was like living on a knife's edge, not knowing from one day to the next what was going to happen. No matter how busy I had been, I had always made time to take her to the library or the hairdressers and to the Post Office to collect her pension so that she could maintain her independence. Gradually, one by one, we had to relinquish these outings, and she had to come to terms with being more dependent upon me to do these things for her.

For quite some time I had had to bath her; but even this was becoming more difficult. Outwardly I was managing to keep everything under control, yet there was a kind of panic building up within me. It was almost unbearable to see my poor Mum deteriorating daily before my eyes, knowing there was nothing to be done for her. She was so courageous and uncomplaining.

We did our best to provide her with every comfort that was possible, and Bernard shared much of the responsibility of caring for her. Fortunately they had a close mother-in-law/son-in-law relationship, and a great affection for each other.

In the early days at Brewster House I had been able to bring Mum across from the flat to join in some of our festivities. Gradually even that became too difficult. So many things were slipping away, time was running out and my professional experience with the elderly did nothing to dispel my fears and impending grief. How could I envisage life without her . . .

This personal stress led me towards a greater understanding of the problems faced by families when caring for an elderly relative. Often the 'carers', many of whom are elderly themselves, have great difficulty in coping without sufficient support. It is not unknown for them to die before the person they are caring for does, because of the enormous strain they are under.

With all this in mind, we used one of our bungalows at Brewster House for short stay care, so that carers could have some occasional respite. Unfortunately, things were made very difficult for us by constant pressure from the Director to keep all beds fully occupied. Of course this was impossible to do in the short stay bungalow as the use of beds had to be flexible to suit the needs of the carers.

Social workers also did not take advantage of short stay for their clients; and requests for long stay always seemed to take priority. It really was an uphill struggle. The lack of support made it very difficult for us to hold on to what we considered to be a very valuable community resource.

Since I was able to empathise with their problems, much of my time was spent in counselling families. It always seemed worse if their loved one was suffering from senile dementia. Often they could not come to terms with the changes that were taking place.

Many times a son or daughter has said to me, 'My mum or dad was never like this; she/he is a totally different person now from the one I have known all my life.' Sometimes they were embarrassed by their loved one's behaviour, and this must be one of the hardest things to accept, especially when your own mother or father does not appear to know you any more, and there is no sign of recognition.

Sometimes it works in reverse and a son or daughter refuses to accept that there is anything wrong with mum or dad. They deny it because it is too painful to face up to. We had such a case at Brewster House.

Kate was in her late seventies, slightly built, with a saucy smile and

Mrs C. In Residence

a twinkle in her eye. She was always joking with the staff, but it soon became apparent that she was trying desperately to cover up for her forgetfulness and confusion.

Kate's only daughter, Mary, was a teacher, in her mid fifties and unmarried. They had a very loving, close relationship. Kate had been widowed when Mary was a small child; and had therefore, had to work hard to support the two of them, especially to see Mary through teacher training college. It had been a hard struggle but Kate was very proud of her Mary.

As time progressed Kate became worse. Sometimes she would sit in her room for hours, getting everything out of the cupboards and drawers and spreading them out on her bed. At other times she would refuse to go to bed and would sit all night long in an armchair. Then she started doing bizarre things at the dining table, and sometimes lying down on the floor in the lounge. Other residents would have to step round her.

Jock, also in his late seventies, lived in the same bungalow as Kate. He was a retired professional man, a dentist, quite badly disabled following two operations on his legs. He walked with crutches, but managed considerably well under the circumstances.

One day Jock came to me to complain about Kate's behaviour. He seemed to think she knew what she was doing and was deliberately annoying everyone. I talked to him as one professional person to another and explained what was happening to Kate so that he would realise she was not responsible for her actions. When he showed signs of understanding, I enlisted his help in trying to persuade the other residents in that bungalow to be less belligerent to Kate and show some compassion.

To give Jock credit, from then on he was absolutely marvellous with Kate, helping her in so many kindly ways. Other residents soon followed his example and the situation became more tolerable for them.

Mary came frequently to take Kate out. She would vehemently deny there was anything odd about her mother's behaviour. Whenever I tried to speak to her about it and suggest ways she might help Kate, she refused to accept there was anything wrong, and indicated it must be something we were doing to upset her mother. Irritably she would retort, 'Mother is always all right when she is with me.' But, of course, we knew this was not so. These outings always made Kate worse; you could see poor Mary was desperately trying to suppress her fears and emotions.

Eventually Kate's condition deteriorated so much that she had to be seen by the psycho-geriatrician. We kept Mary informed and again tried to help her to come to terms with what was happening; reassuring her that we were all fond of Kate and would do our utmost to manage her at Brewster House for as long as possible.

Even at that stage she would only admit that Kate was 'a bit confused', and voiced her disapproval of the specialist's visit by stating, 'I will take mum home and look after her myself.' This was out of the question of course. She was obviously not thinking rationally.

'No way could Kate be left all day while you are out at school, Mary, and you would have no respite whatever,' I whispered, touching her hand gently. The breakthrough came immediately upon the impact of our physical contact. She looked up at me; slowly tears welled into her eyes and rolled down her cheeks silently. She strangled a sob as I held her hand . . .

Kate died a few months later. There was no funeral as she had bequeathed her body to medical science. Poor Mary's grief must have been suspended in mid-air, as she had to forego that essential opportunity to mourn.

We sent her a beautiful indoor plant, with a note expressing our sympathy. It was important for her to know that we cared and understood her sorrow. A few weeks later we received a letter from her, thanking us for the plant, for our kindness to her and for the loving care we had given to Kate.

Witnessing the anguish of people such as Mary, often made me thankful that my mother was not senile. Although physically very ill, she was still mentally alert. Senile dementia must be one of the saddest and most difficult conditions to cope with, and something many of us fear in old age. Since it is a disease that can affect so many of us either directly or indirectly in our lives, the Authorities must provide more specialist care for the sufferers, and adequate support for the carers.

There was a slow start in building relationships with the local community at Brewster House. People had been used to a certain image of Old People's Homes, and could not understand our new philosophy. It took a long time and much talking to get them to grasp the fact that our residents did not wish to be patronised. Well meaning people can unintentionally do more harm than good on occasions. A particular case comes to mind.

Tom was very disabled, his breathing laboured, his heart weak, and he had great difficulty in walking. Nevertheless, he was a fiercely independent man. Whilst longing to go out, he was too proud to be seen in a wheelchair. It took weeks of skilful persuasion on our part to get him to agree on an outing to the village shops in a wheelchair.

The special day came, Tom sat back in his chair with a rug round his legs, warm and comfortable, ready to enjoy his outing. Eva, one of our new care assistants, called a cheery, 'We're off now, Mrs Chamberlain,' and waved goodbye.

Within ten minutes they were back, Tom red-faced and very angry. Eva, a tremor in her voice, hardly paused for breath as she related what had happened.

'We just got down to the village, Mrs C, when some lady stopped to speak to us. She patted Tom on his head as if he were a dog being taken for "walkies" and spoke to him as if he were a child. Poor old Tom was furious and demanded to be brought back because he felt so humiliated.'

What a catastrophe that had turned out to be! We were back to square one again, and it took many more weeks before Tom could be encouraged to venture out again. That lady probably thought she was being kind in stopping to talk to Tom and Eva that fateful day. If only her approach had been less condescending it could have been a pleasant exchange between neighbours.

The only good thing to come out of that particular incident was that when Eva took Tom out she had addressed me as Mrs Chamberlain; but in her flurry to relate everything on their return, she called me 'Mrs C.' I always felt a particular pleasure when new staff suddenly referred to me as 'Mrs C.' for it meant we had reached a comfortable stage in our relationship.

Thankfully, the Tom and Eva incident was an isolated one. Eventually we made many friends in the neighbourhood, some of whom invited residents out to local events, and provided the transport. Once they appreciated our emphasis on the 'quality of life' and could see the results, there was much goodwill and co-operation on both sides.

Often members of the public and other colleagues would query, 'What happens when some of your residents deteriorate with old age and become too frail to do anything for themselves?' My response was to make it clear that in those circumstances we increased our caring role without finding it necessary to abandon our basic philosophy. No matter how dependent residents eventually became, we were still sensitive to their needs as individuals and did our utmost to protect their dignity and self-respect.

During the later part of my career many residents did not take long to reach that stage, since on admission they were already confused, incontinent, very weak and frail, often with diminishing hearing and sight (and sometimes all of these and more). Our task of encouraging self-help in small group living became increasingly difficult.

There has always been, and I daresay there always will be, the problem of some old folk themselves expecting and demanding everything to be done for them. Having been conditioned by over-caring families or others, they feel it is their right in old age to be totally cosseted and dependent, frequently resorting to emotional blackmail to achieve the desired result. As professionals we become used to such attitudes and work towards positive and acceptable change.

The problems now, however, facing residential staff are due in part to the current emphasis on community care, and not entirely because people are living to a much greater age. Old folk can now stay in their own homes much longer with the support of services such as Home Helps, Meals on Wheels, Domiciliary Care Assistants, Day Care, Good Neighbours and similar schemes. Unfortunately, the authorities are not always able to provide sufficient resources to give vulnerable, lonely old people the degree of care they need, or to protect them from abuse by uncaring families so it is not working as well as it might.

Given the opportunity, most of us would prefer to stay in our own home for as long as possible, so one cannot blame the old folk for choosing to do so, but the repercussions for residential staff are quite demoralising. When a situation does break down and a person is admitted to a Home, it is viewed as a 'last resort' rather than the planned, positive experience it was intended to be.

If this trend continues I foresee many changes in residential Homes for the Elderly, with the marrying of the Health Authority and Social Services. Many private establishments now function as part Nursing Home and part Residential Home and therefore have to be registered with the Health Authority and Social Services. This means that qualified nurses are also employed to complement residential staff.

Whatever the future holds for the elderly, it is to be hoped that the 'powers that be' and all the carers, realise that 'Old people are not a separate race, come down from outer space.' They do not want to be treated differently from other members of the community, but to be part of it. Considering the price they have paid to society, we have a moral obligation to provide them with the best quality of care.

In the early days one of the biggest frustrations was the constant battle against jealous criticism from staff in other Homes. They would often be heard to say, 'Oh yes. They can do all these things at Brewster House because they don't have such frail and disabled residents as we have.' Or 'Well they're lucky; they have a lovely new building,' and similar remarks. They also appeared to imagine that all our achievements had come about by some miracle, no matter how much we tried to explain otherwise. Usually this attitude was overcome by inviting them to spend some time in Brewster House to see for themselves that our residents were no different from theirs, and discover how we went about our work. Most of them left with a very changed attitude, having learned much that could be implemented in their own Homes, even if they did not have the benefit of our facilities.

I was always the first to acknowledge that we were fortunate to have such a marvellous new building. But experience had taught me that much could be done to improve the vital 'quality' of life for residents, even in older buildings; but this required the right attitude from the staff.

The ignorance that abounded among colleagues who should have known better, really made me bristle at times, and it was very tiring having constantly to do battle to defend one's principles. One does not expect 'Care' to be uniform in every residential establishment, as there are varying demands which require a range of flexible provision. Nevertheless the failure of so many to readily identify aspects of good practice must be cause for concern.

CHAPTER XVIII

Whilst I was fully occupied with implementing these progressive practices at work, my private life was becoming more fraught every day. I could not neglect my dear Mum so there was never any discontinuation of my caring role. She had also had a couple of emergency admissions to hospital during this time, causing us grave concern; once having had a stroke from which she miraculously recovered.

Added to this, Bernard had to go into hospital for a second major operation on his hand; the first one the previous year having been unsuccessful. How could I possibly manage my work, travel to London each day to visit Bernard, and look after Mum at the same time?

Our son, Steven had married when we were at Warner House. He and our lovely daughter-in-law, Vyvienne, offered to help. But they were both social workers with very demanding jobs, specialising in child care, having to work all kinds of unsocial hours including night duty. Whilst they were always thoughtful and helped whenever possible – for Steven loved his Nan dearly – I was reluctant to place more responsibility on their shoulders than was absolutely necessary.

I decided to apply for some help from social services myself, after first discussing things with my mother to ascertain her approval. The request was for Mum to have a two week short stay in one of our local Homes, while Bernard was in hospital. After this was duly processed and arrangements finalised, my initial reaction was relief, knowing Mum would not be on her own if anything should happen to her while

I was out.

Nevertheless, when the time came to take her to the Home, I suddenly experienced a terrible pang of guilt. What was I doing, putting my mother in a Home? What could I be thinking of? It seemed I was about to find out at first hand, how other loving daughters must have felt when their mothers were admitted to one of my Homes.

At first I battled desperately to shut out the guilt feelings, but they just would not go away. Panic and indecision followed swiftly. 'I can't go through with it,' I told myself. Fearing I might do something foolish, I searched my dear Mum's face. She was accepting the situation, with a concern for me that was as great as mine was for her. If she could be so brave about it, why was I going to pieces?

Immediately, common sense took over again. Realising it was the most sensible course to take in the circumstances, we proceeded as planned. Still, I was anxious to assure Mum that it would not be for long, and that I would pop across to see her every day, if only for a brief visit. Steven and Vyvienne also promised to call in as often as possible, between visits to Bernard, too, of course.

It was so important to let her know that she was still loved and would not be forgotten. She was also very concerned about Bernard, so I agreed to let her know how he was as soon as I could after his operation. Eventually it worked out satisfactorily, although I must confess that to this day I still feel a certain kind of guilt, which really has no rationality about it. How much worse it must be for other caring families, when admission to a Home has to be considered on a permanent basis.

One of the important roles of residential staff is to help families work through their feelings of guilt in such situations. My personal experience showed me the importance of this; and it was something often included in training sessions with staff.

Thankfully we had come through our family crisis reasonably unscathed, and Bernard was soon fit to return to school again. Unfortunately his second operation turned out to be no more successful than the first, which was very disappointing.

As time passed, personal responsibilities coupled with the demands of my work, began to take their toll. A feeling of tension was building up inside me, and I am sure that some of that tension was passed on to my dear Mum, with a sharp word and a show of impatience now and again. Oh! how bitterly one regrets these things later on; more feelings of guilt to come to terms with. My only consolation was the knowledge that my Mum loved me and understood the strain I was under. She would have forgiven me for what is, after all, a human reaction when one has suffered continual emotional worry and stress over a long period.

Towards the end of my second year at Brewster House, my mother was admitted to hospital for the last time. We all knew that the end was near. After a couple of weeks when it did not seem possible she could hold on any longer, she opened her eyes and asked me what day it was.

'Monday, Mum,' I replied in a whisper as I held her hand.

After a few more minutes she opened her eyes again and enquired what the date was. '25th July,' I told her.

Two days later, on the 27th July 1983, she slipped into a coma. As I sat clasping her hand, tears surged up obscuring my vision. The date was of great significance; it was our shared birthday. We had always celebrated it together. When she had asked the date a couple of days earlier, she must have been determined to be with me still on our special day.

My pain was unbearable. 'Please Mum, don't leave me,' I begged. 'How could I ever face another birthday without you?'

Bernard came into the room just as she drew her final breath. At last she was at peace. I had never before cried so uncontrollably. How strange that she should have brought me into the world so many years before on her birthday, and should now leave the world herself on that very same date years later!

Bernard put his arm round me comfortingly, allowing me to cry myself dry. He understood my sorrow as only he could. For the next few days everything appeared unreal, and I felt terribly restless. It was not so bad while I was at work, but immediately I came home to the flat and realised Mum was not there, I would start weeping.

It was impossible to sort out her belongings in her bedroom. 'That task will have to wait,' I told myself, 'until I have the strength to face up to it.' Somehow strength and courage did come to the fore when I was with Steven. He had taken his Nan's death very hard, and also needed to be comforted.

On the day of the funeral everything was all right until the hearse drew up and I saw mother's coffin. My legs were rooted motionless at the door, just as they had been at Dad's funeral. Only this time it was much worse. Mum was not there to hold and comfort me, for it was she who was in that coffin. It seemed so final; I would never see her again.

Clinging to the frame of the door, I sobbed my heart out and no one could persuade me to move until the Vicar, who was accompanying us came over, put his arm around my shoulder and gently guided me to one of the waiting cars.

As a family we all wept unashamedly at the funeral. We had all loved her so much, and knew she would be sorely missed. Grief and sorrow completely overwhelmed us.

When we returned to the flat to have some refreshment, I was chatting to the Vicar when quite suddenly I lost my voice and couldn't speak. Thankfully there was no need to worry about my work as I had decided to take a few weeks leave owing to me. Bernard who was on holiday from school, suggested we go to our caravan, nestling in a beautiful, peaceful spot in the Sussex Downs. As we had been unable to go there for a long time, he thought the rest and change would be particularly beneficial.

Content enough with this proposal, I really made an effort to pull myself together, knowing how worried Bernard was. But with the passing days, my voice had still not returned. It was a peculiar feeling, giving me an insight into the difficulties of not being able to communicate. It was eerie for Bernard too, as he was unable to have any conversation with me. We had to depend on sign language and writing notes to each other.

After more than a week of this, Bernard suggested we should go to see the local doctor. He was an elderly man, rather dapper in appearance, with greying hair and a thin moustache. Bernard explained about my loss of voice and told him of our recent bereavement.

Thoughtfully, he sat for a while, tapping his fingers on the desk. Having decided what to advise, he looked at Bernard, 'Your wife has had a shock, and what she must do is talk about it. That's the only thing to do; she must talk about it. It will do no good for her to bottle things up.'

Listening to this I could hardly believe what I was hearing. 'Silly old fool,' I thought angrily. 'How can I talk about things if I've lost my voice? That's what I came to see him about.'

After ten days of enforced silence, Bernard decided to pop outside one morning to clean the car. Pottering around in the caravan, I was doing some little jobs whilst listening to the radio. Music was being played and I suddenly joined in singing. It was strange at first to hear my own voice; then I just whooped with joy. Having always done a lot of singing and entertaining, it seemed to come naturally that I should sing at first, rather than speak.

Delighted to have regained my voice, I went outside, crept quietly up behind Bernard and tapped him on the shoulder. As he turned round to look at me, I intoned slowly and distinctly, 'The rain in Spain stays mainly in the plain.'

He looked so relieved, and stepping back in mock surprise he threw his arms up in the air as he responded, 'By jove, she's got it!'

We grabbed each other and did a little dance. Luckily nobody was about at the time, or we would surely have been carted off to the nearest mental institution. Our natural sense of humour soon took over, and for the first time since Mum's death we were actually laughing, particularly when we recalled that visit to the doctor. It seemed strange to begin with, because I had been unable to imagine myself ever laughing again.

Of course, there have been many times since, especially in the early days, when something has happened to remind me of Mum, and I have felt a lump in my throat and the stinging of tears in my eyes. When we visited Devon on our first holiday after she died, we were resting on a seat at the top of some cliffs, looking out to sea. It was a beautiful sunny day. One moment I was happily admiring the scene, then instantly I was completely overcome with grief.

Bernard wondered what was wrong, and through tears and sniffles I blurted out, 'This is the first holiday I shall not be able to send Mum a card or take her home a little present.'

On another occasion I had a totally different emotion. Old habits seemed hard to break, after caring for Mum for such a long time, and when shopping I would often cater still for the three of us. One day I bought some lamb chops, her favourite. About to cook them, it dawned on me that she was not there. I felt angry. It was just as if she had died deliberately to avoid my cooking. How irrational are reactions in bereavement.

Fortunately I have since reached the stage where I can talk about Mum and all the things she used to say and do, in quite a natural and healthy way. Learning by experience how devastating the loss of a loved one can be, has enabled me, through my work, to do quite a lot of bereavement counselling.

There are times, of course, when I still miss Mum dreadfully, especially on that certain occasion every year – our shared birthday. It was such a special day for the two of us, and somehow there is then an overwhelming desire to be close to her. A visit to the crematorium chapel to see her name in the Book of Remembrance, is a great comfort to me.

About six months after Mum's death, just as we were managing to become used to our grief and things returned to normal, Bernard was suddenly taken very ill with a heart attack. We were spending a few days at our bungalow in Essex at the time.

Following the speeding ambulance to the hospital in my car, I remember repeating over and over to myself, 'Dear God, not Bernard, too. Please, dear God . . . no . . .'

CHAPTER XIX

It was touch and go with Bernard for the first few days. Steven and I spent many hours at his bedside, silently praying that he would not be taken from us. Our prayers were answered when, after ten days, he had recovered sufficiently to be allowed home. With dedicated nursing care and many 'Get Well' wishes from friends and colleagues, he somehow found the strength to cling to life and hold on.

Bernard was not allowed to return to school for three months, when he went back for only one term before taking early retirement, much to my relief. His school held a big retirement 'do' for him, to which Steven, Vyvienne and I were invited. We felt very proud of him, for he was obviously popular and highly respected. Children and staff would miss him.

For some time one of my ambitions had been to produce a quarterly magazine within the Home, written for and by staff, residents, their families and friends. Following a discussion about this idea at a staff meeting, we decided to have a go.

So the 'Brewster House Times' came into being; the day it was launched was very exciting for all of us. The magazine contained information and news about the Home, plus articles, stories, food recipes, jokes, gardening tips and many other items. The most entertaining stories were those told by the old folk themselves; memories of their lives when they were young, humorous and sad. It was interesting to read about a world totally different from the one we know today.

To my mind, that was one of the most important aspects of the magazine. It seemed a marvellous opportunity to record the memoirs of our present generation of elderly people, which would otherwise have been lost for ever. Many of the residents were in their late eighties and nineties, in some cases having outlived their sons and daughters, who if they were still alive, were often elderly themselves.

One gem of a story in the magazine was told by an old chap who was a real East Ender -

The Hard but Happy Times When I was a Young Man
by Harry Brown.

I was brought up in Hackney. When I left school, just after the First World War times were very hard. My first job was in a factory working on a drilling machine. That was the start of many jobs.

I worked in a bottle factory for a pound a week, and then a piano factory for a pound a week. They would only take you on if they were busy, so you were out when things got slack, and it was off around the streets as a rag and bone man to get a few shillings for my mother (she was a widow with no income). I also went around the streets with a wheelbarrow selling salt at twopence a lump, and vinegar at twopence a pint; stone for cleaning doorsteps was one penny for two pieces. If it rained that was the job finished for the day. I worked in the markets around Hackney.

Things started to look up for me when my sister loaned me ten pounds to start my own business going around the streets selling vegetables on a horse and cart. That lasted about sixteen years. To make a bit of extra money I used to go to the market and buy a few wild birds and train them to sing, and within a few weeks I would sell them as singing birds.

Then I started a coffee shop, but that did not last long – that went broke. Then I got a job in the building game as a painter, I knew nothing about painting, but I got by. That job did not last long, so it was out on the streets again looking for work. There was no jumping in cars then, it was a case of shanking it (walking).

I married at twenty-six years old, and started married life in one room in my mother's house, and my little family of three (one daughter and two sons). It was a case of getting a home of our own.

People don't know how well off they are today. If anybody roughed it – I did.

Harry Brown

That was just one of the interesting tales I cherish from the 'Brewster House Times'. Of course, producing the magazine was very time consuming, but it did give us all a great deal of pleasure; a very worthwhile project.

When Bernard had been retired for about nine months, I began to toy with the idea of following suit. Good foundations had been laid at the Home and there was no reason why that should not continue, I thought to myself. I might even be able to fulfil my other ambition and write a book about my life and experiences in residential work. Somehow, now seemed to be the right time to go.

After much soul searching, I finally made up my mind and handed in my three months' notice to leave at the end of July 1985. Everyone seemed genuinely sorry I was going, and we expected a great deal of emotional upheaval during those last three months.

Brewster House had become my baby, and it was my fervent hope that whoever was my successor, would take care of it for me. How delighted I was when my previous Deputy, Joan, applied for the post and was appointed. All my fears dissolved for I knew that my baby would be in safe hands for the time being at least, for who knows what the future holds? It was a tremendous relief.

In the last week leading up to my retirement, Bernard and I were invited to a special tea with the residents, held in my honour. The old folk presented me with many gifts. It was both a sad and happy occasion. Some of the residents cried when they kissed me goodbye, and that was heartbreaking. How could I leave them? Fretting inwardly, my emotions in a turmoil, I had a strange feeling that I was letting them down or abandoning them.

On my last day at the Home, there was another retirement celebration, this time with staff and other close colleagues. Bernard, Steven and Vyvienne were also invited, making the occasion very special for me. Mrs Turner, from County Hall, was there, too. This also gave me particular pleasure, as we had always had a good working relationship and a great respect for each other.

During my retirement speech, I felt moved to turn to my family and express my appreciation for their encouragement and support over the years. Without that from one's family, residential work must be nigh impossible. I had indeed been fortunate with my partner, for my long and irregular hours had undoubtedly taken its toll of our social life. Yet Bernard never complained. He accepted that it was my job, and I shall always be grateful for his patience.

Phillip, my Deputy, had organised the event according to my wishes, and Maggie, our super Bursar, had arranged an attractive buffet, making it a very memorable occasion for me. They really did me proud, and gave me many useful presents to enjoy in my retirement. Travelling home in the car, I sensed the collective voice of the staff echoing round and round in my head, 'Goodbye, Mrs C. All the best.' Apprehensively I wondered how I would adjust to this new phase in my life.

About a week later a most amazing coincidence occurred. Bernard happened to be reading a local newspaper sent by his former school secretary, when a heading above one of the articles caught his eye: 'Served Old Folk for Thirty Years' it proclaimed, followed by an account which read:

> Millicent Liam – known as Millie – has retired after thirty years

working as a Care Assistant. Since its opening in 1964, she has been at George Moore Lodge, Old People's Home. She said she will always have happy memories of her work there. "I could write a book on the thousands of different experiences that I've had here, both funny and sad. I've been here since the beginning and seen all the changes.

In 1964 the residents were people who happened to be old. Now, in 1985, they need much more help. Maybe, now that I've retired, I'll finally get the time to write it all down."

A special party was held to mark her retirement when she was presented with many gifts by the Mayor and Mayoress on behalf of the residents and staff. They also thanked her for the care that she had given to old people in the borough.

Miss Liam will shortly be taking a holiday in her Welsh homeland, and she will probably move there permanently next year.

I experienced a strange sensation as Bernard handed the newspaper for me to read. It was, of course, our own dear Millie, with whom I had lost touch during the latter part of my career. Not only did we share the same birth date, but unbeknown to each other we had both decided to retire at exactly the same time, and expressed an intention to write about our experiences.

Life certainly does have some strange twists and turns, I thought to myself; remarking to Bernard, 'Let's hope Millie does write her memoirs for it would make interesting reading. From her angle she had seen many changes in one establishment, over the years.'

How delightful it would be to see Millie again, for she was a truly unforgettable character. Perhaps one day it will be possible; I do hope so.

This incident recalled to mind reminiscences of Arthur, too. We had always kept in touch, but how good it would be to see him again after so many years.

'Now that we have the time,' I suggested to Bernard, 'we must go to visit Arthur and Dorothy. It's unlikely they will know about Millie's retirement, so we can take the newspaper cutting to show them.'

A week later, following a phone call to a delighted Arthur and Dorothy we were on our way to spend a few days with them. It was good to have the time to visit old friends. This was undoubtedly one of the benefits of retirement. Until then I had felt as if I were at home on extended leave; it all seemed rather unreal.

Travelling along in the car, my thoughts spanned the years. What would Arthur think about the changes that have taken place in many Homes, I wondered. Even in the area of routine, essential matters such as residents' pensions, laundry and incontinence, great differences had evolved.

A scale of charges is laid down by the local authority, according to a person's means. In the majority of cases a certain amount is deducted from the weekly pension, which goes towards the cost of a resident's accommodation. The rest is given back for personal spending. For residents on basic retirement pension, obviously the charges are subsidised.

At George Moore Lodge 'pocket money' was paid out weekly, with the residents filing in, one by one, to the lounge where Arthur or I and the clerk would be sitting at a table. We would issue the appropriate money to each resident, which included a small allowance, from the authority, for 'tobacco and sweets'; a hangover from the Poor Law. Then they would sign a form as proof of receipt. What a degrading experience that must have been for old folk, to have to queue up like that, but that was the accepted procedure then.

At The Oak Tree and Warner House, I ruled that each resident's pocket money should be put in a sealed envelope with an individual name on the outside. We then visited all the lounges, giving each person his or her envelope, whilst they signed the form attached to a clip-board. This made the method much more personal and less humiliating. Thankfully the 'sweet and tobacco' allowance had long since been discontinued.

In the early days at Brewster House, an experiment was carried out whereby residents cashed their own pensions at the Post Office and were then responsible for paying their own accommodation charges. Unfortunately the Post Office was at the far end of the village, with quite a steep hill to negotiate. The Home had no transport of its own, so staff had to escort the old folk, many of whom had to be pushed in wheelchairs.

This became too time-consuming for the staff, and exhausting. Reluctantly we had to abandon that idea, and revert to the tried and tested arrangements I had adopted at the previous Homes. However, we made one significant change. The reference to 'pocket money' was altered to 'personal allowance', which seemed a much more suitable description.

At George Moore Lodge, no laundry was done on the premises, other than the sluicing of incontinent linen and clothing or hand washing of stockings and such like. There were no washing machines, so all the laundry had to be listed and packed in big canvas sacks to be sent out. Clean washing had to be checked and sorted on its return. It was never satisfactory, as inevitably there would be shortages or clothing and linen would have been ruined.

At The Oak Tree there was a washing machine and drier, so the care assistants did some of the residents' clothing on the premises; the rest was sent out with the linen to be laundered.

Warner House had better facilities. A full-time laundress took good care of the residents' clothing, and all the laundry, except soiled linen, was done on the premises. This was a considerable improvement as it provided a much more personal service for the residents.

Brewster House also had good facilities, including a special machine for soiled linen, although it was more difficult to cope with all the laundry there, because the staff establishment did not allow for a laundress. Some of the domestic hours had to be used, which was not very satisfactory, but the only alternative to sending out laundry, which we did not want to do.

We managed somehow. Some of the residents were encouraged to use the little laundry room in their bungalows to wash out their own clothing. A few were able to do this alone after being shown how to use the equipment; others had the help of staff. It was useful therapy, but unfortunately much of it eventually had to be undertaken by staff, as residents gradually became too frail to cope.

From my Oak Tree days, there was an improvement in dealing with incontinence. We worked on the premise that prevention is better than cure, without meekly accepting that a person was irreversibly incontinent and that nothing could be done. The GPs were requested to try and diagnose the cause of the problem, to find out if it was caused by stress or some physical malfunction that could be treated. Only after all avenues had been exhausted did we admit that it was irreversible, and work out a sensitive management programme in private with the resident.

At Brewster House the subject of incontinence was discussed frequently in training sessions. Staff agreed it was important to help people maintain their dignity and self respect. It was much less time-consuming to quietly remind a patient to pop along to the toilet at prearranged times, hopefully avoiding an 'accident', than was the unpleasant task of cleaning up when it was too late.

By doing this, it was often possible to keep a person dry and comfortable, and save them from what might otherwise be embarrassing situations.

I was jolted out of my reverie when Bernard remarked that we had almost reached our destination. Inwardly I felt like an excited child. How lovely it would be to see Arthur again. How many years had it been? I couldn't remember. My thoughts were all jumbled up. But one thing was certain: we would have plenty to talk about.

CHAPTER XX

We received a very warm welcome from Dorothy and Arthur. They were obviously delighted to see us, and for the first couple of hours none of us paused for breath, as there was so much news to catch up on. We worked out that it had been eight years since we had seen each other.

Over the next few days we talked about many things. As I had predicted, Arthur was truly amazed at the changes that had taken place in residential work since his retirement. Interspersed with this, there was much laughter when we recalled some amusing incidents at George Moore Lodge, such as the day when Mr and Mrs Jones were admitted.

Although crippled with arthritis, they were a smart looking couple in their mid-seventies. We had gone to great pains to provide a double room for them. How were we to know (for these were the days when we had very little information) that they did not get on well together, and had not even slept in the same room for years. Our first intimation of this was when their son came to visit them. Arthur and I burst out laughing, for we could see the funny side of it.

'Well, there isn't much we can do about it now,' I said. 'There's no other room available. We'll have to take a chance that they get on well together. Perhaps they'll have a second honeymoon,' I chuckled.

Indeed, for the first few weeks, this did appear to be the case, and Mr and Mrs Jones were quite lovey dovey, that is until they fell out. Then they would have a terrible slanging match and not speak to each other for days. Obviously this was their way of going on, and we left

Mrs C. In Residence

them to it, as we had no right to interfere.

One day their son, Bert, came in to tell us it would soon be his parents' Golden Wedding Anniversary. They had spoken to him about it and had requested a big celebration in the Home to be shared with everyone. Bert asked our permission for this and, of course, we agreed, although we were somewhat surprised in the circumstances.

When the great day came, we made a special effort to prepare the dining room for a slap-up reception. All the residents were seated and many VIPs were in attendance, including the Mayor. Cook had made a Golden Wedding cake, and the tables looked really attractive. A lady sat at the piano, ready to play the Wedding March when Mr and Mrs Jones entered the room. All eyes were set, looking towards the door, waiting for them.

'Here they come,' someone shouted. The music started playing and everyone clapped and sang, 'For They Are Jolly Good Fellows', as Mr and Mrs Jones swept into the room, arm in arm. Both looked radiantly happy and were obviously enjoying all the fuss.

Suddenly, between entering the room and walking to their place on the other side of the table, they had one of their quarrels. From then on they even refused to sit next to each other. We couldn't believe what we were seeing when Mr Jones stormed to the opposite side of the room and sat down, glaring across at his wife.

It was another of those farcical situations. Here were we, with glasses poised, ready to toast the happy couple's health, and they weren't even speaking!

Arthur and Dorothy were also amused by something that happened when I was at The Oak Tree. A concert party came to entertain the residents. Everything was going fine until the baritone got up and started singing, 'Some Enchanted Evening'. Bertha, a sixty-eight year old resident, suddenly shot up out of her seat. Standing facing him, she mimed all the words as he sang. Not content with that, she began flailing her arms in the air, reaching out to him in exaggerated gestures, depicting a romantic duo between two lovers.

Other residents hissed to her, 'Sit down,' but she seemed oblivious to everyone except that handsome baritone, who was singing for her alone. Just as I was about to make my way along the gangway and ask her to sit down, the singer finished, and thankfully so did she.

The poor man had a mixed kind of expression as he hurriedly retreated from the room, stifling laughter that was tinged with embarrassment. How he had even managed to finish the song, I'll never know.

'We often wondered what possessed Bertha to make such an exhibition of herself,' I mused. 'Perhaps she was a frustrated actress. Still, ever since that incident, whenever I hear "Some Enchanted Evening" being sung, a vision of Bertha appears before me, causing me to laugh and wince at the same time.'

Following our visit to Arthur, retirement became more of a reality to me. It had done me good to go back to my roots again, and recall so many things that had happened throughout my career. It was just the incentive needed to begin writing it all down.

One thing I have learned since retirement, is the importance of keeping as busy and active as possible, for it can be all too easy to fall into a lethargic trap. However, I do appreciate being able to do things more at my own pace, without the pressures and demands that residential work always made; although I would not have had it any other way.

Being sixty years of age and a pensioner took some getting used to at first. Somehow we never imagine ourselves reaching that stage, never seeing ourselves as others see us. During the past year, Bernard and I have visited many friends we had not seen for a long while, and could not fail to notice how much older they looked. They probably thought the same about us, because we are all older. It's just that it is more difficult to perceive in oneself.

Irrational as it may seem, there have been times when it didn't feel right to enjoy my new found leisure while others were still having to work. But thankfully, with the passing of time that feeling is receding.

Quite recently, I was treated in a very patronising manner by a young lady of whom I was making an enquiry. Needless to say, by the time I had finished explaining to her the folly of her ways, she probably wished she hadn't spoken at all. It is to be hoped that she learned something from that incident. Why does the attitude of some people change, immediately they know you are over sixty?

On the whole, Bernard and I have adjusted very well to retirement. Being fortunate in having many varied interests including voluntary work, enabling us to continue using our appropriate skills, life is still meaningful. There are many, of course, who are unable to enjoy their retirement because of loneliness, loss of status and social contacts, disability, low income – sometimes a combination of all these factors. So we are grateful for what we have, and do not take anything for granted.

Deep down inside of me there is frequently a feeling of desperation, as if time is running out and there is still so much to do. I expect this is common as one travels along the path to old age. In my case it is probably emphasized by my experiences in seeing the worst effects of the ageing process. At times such as this, I talk to myself quite severely, to get things into perspective, because there are many old people living full and contented lives.

Thinking I would never see my dear mother again was also wrong; for every time I look in a mirror, she smiles back at me. With every passing year I grow more like her . . .

Reflecting on my career, it is with deep gratitude that I remember the many staff, for their loyalty and hard work. Also I recall with pleasure, the privilege of having had in my care so many unforgettable characters, who taught me so much about life, and death. However relationships are a two-way thing, and I like to think that their lives may have been made a little brighter by knowing me.

Over the years, people often asked, 'How can you work with old people? It must be so depressing.'

With a grin, I would retort, 'How often do you have to tell a sixty-five year old the facts of life, or be a mediator between a married couple at their Golden Wedding?'

What was that? 'Old Mr Smith has set fire to the waste paper basket again. Will someone fetch Mrs C?'

'Coming, girls, coming . . .'